How Do Journalists Think?

A Proposal for the Study of Cognitive Bias in Newsmaking

S. Holly Stocking
Indiana University

Paget H. Gross
Columbia University

1989

ERIC Clearinghouse on Reading and Communication Skills

Smith Research Center
Indiana University

2805 E. 10th Street, Suite 150
Bloomington, IN 47405

Acknowledgements

Published 1989 by:

ERIC Clearinghouse on Reading and Communication Skills
Carl B. Smith, Director
Smith Research Center, Suite 150
2805 East 10th Street
Indiana University
Bloomington, Indiana 47405

Typesetting and design at ERIC/RCS and printing by Indiana University Printing Services.

This publication was prepared with funding from the Office of Educational Research and Improvement, U.S. Department of Education, under contract no. RI88062001. Contractors undertaking such projects under government sponsorship are encouraged to express freely their judgment in professional and technical matters. Points of view or opinions, however, do not necessarily represent the official view or opinions of the Office of Educational Research and Improvement.

For information on reprinting portions of this monograph, contact S. Holly Stocking, School of Journalism, Indiana University, Bloomington, IN 47407.

Library of Congress Cataloging-in-Publication Data
Stocking, S. Holly, 1945-

How Do Journalists Think?
A Proposal for the Study of Cognitive Bias in Newsmaking

Includes bibliographical references.

1. Journalists—Psychology. 2. Selectivity (Psychology). 3. Journalism—Psychological aspects. 4. Cognition. 5. Journalism—Decision making. 6. Journalism—Social aspects. I. Gross, Paget H., 1956- . II. Title.

PN4749.S86 1989   020.4'01'9   89-23433

ISBN 0-927516-03-9

Table of Contents

Preface vii

I. Media Bias, Cognitive Bias? 1

II. Cognitive Processes in Journalism: An Overview 7

    Categorization 8

    Theory Generation 10

    Theory Testing 10

    Selection of Information 10

    Integration of Information 11

III. Categorization 13

    Labeling 14

    Inference 16

    Judgment 17

IV. Theory Generation 19

    Content of Theories 20

    Variations in Complexity and Stability 21

    Expert-Novice Differences 23

V. Theory Testing 27

    One Theory at a Time 27

    Confirmation Bias 27

        Sourcing 28

        Questioning 29

        Handling of Sources 31

        Responding to the Raised Question 32

VI.   Selection of Information 35

    Preference for Theory-Consistent Information 35

        Saliency Biases 39

        Anecdotal versus Base-Rate Information 40

    Preference for Eyewitness Information 42

        Biases in Perceptions of Risk 43

VII. Integration of Information 45

    Causal Linking of Events 45

        Illusory Correlation 46

        The Tendency to Oversimplify the Explanation
        of Complex Events 46

        The Fundamental Attribution Error 47

    Reconstruction and Hindsight Biases 50

    Concluding the Search 53

VIII. Interactions and Perseverance of Biases and Errors 55

IX.   Implications for the Study of Newswork 57

    Research on How Journalists Process Information 58

        Journalists' Categorizations 58

        Journalists' Theories 58

        Effects of Hypotheses and Assumptions
        on Newsgathering 62

        Do Confirmational Strategies Lead to Error? 67

        Selection Biases 69

        Biases in Information Integration 69

    Research on Effects of Environmental Factors
    on Information Processing 69

        Effects of Organizational Constraints 70

        Effects of News Sources, Community
        Structure, and Culture 71

      Effects of Journalistic Norms and Practices 73

      Other Research Needs: Are Biases and Errors
      Amenable to Change? 76

      A Word on Method 79

X.   Summary and Conclusions 85

     Endnotes 89

     References 95

     Appendix 111

     Name Index 115

S. Holly Stocking

is an assistant professor of journalism at Indiana University in Bloomington. Prior to becoming an academic, she worked as a reporter for the *Los Angeles Times*, the *Minneapolis Tribune*, and the Associated Press, among others.

Paget H. Gross

is a student at the Columbia University law school. Prior to studying law, she was an assistant professor of psychology at Indiana University in Bloomington.

Preface

In recent years, cognitive scientists have generated an impressive body of new knowledge about how people think. Much of this research has great potential relevance for the practice and study of newsmaking. However, very little has found its way into investigations of newswork.

The reasons for this oversight are not clear. However, it cannot be that cognitive research is unknown to mass media scholars. Indeed, in recent years, cognitive insights have begun dramatically to transform studies that track the effects of the mass media on news consumers. Why then the relative inattention to this body of knowledge in studies of news producers?

There is some reason to believe that "effects" researchers have embraced this body of knowledge whereas "newswork" researchers have not because of differences in prevailing assumptions in the two lines of investigation. In effects research, the prevailing assumption is that audience members are active consumers of information. They are not automatically affected by news media. Quite the contrary, news consumers are assumed to be affected in very different ways depending on a host of factors, including their original knowledge about a subject, their attitudes and beliefs. Audiences, in short, do not passively receive media messages, but actively transform them in ways well known to cognitive scientists.

In newswork research, by contrast, the prevailing assumption is that individual journalists have very little to say about what eventually becomes news. Indeed, journalists—quite unlike members of their audience—are seen as profoundly constrained by their environments (including the organizations for which they work) such that their personal knowledge about a subject, their attitudes and beliefs have relatively little to contribute to the news.

This emphasis on environmental constraints has been important to our understanding of newsmaking. But it may also have led some investigators to assume that cognitive science, with its assumption that individuals actively transform information, has little of value to contribute. As a colleague recently observed, "Cognitive theories may be interesting, but I bet they only account for a very small proportion of the variance in journalists' behavior."[1]

It is a working assumption of this manuscript that recent work in cognitive science, far from having little of value to contribute, has a great deal to offer to studies of newswork. Although cognitive psychologists and other cognitive scientists tend to study individuals divorced from context, they do NOT, as we shall see, assume that cognitions are idiosyncratic or independent of context; as any thoughtful psychologist will tell you, cognitions can be shared and they can be shaped by environmental forces.

In addition, it might be argued that we can never truly understand the influence of environmental constraints without understanding the mediating role of cognitions. As Dutch researcher Teun van Dijk has forcefully argued in his book on news discourse, "...it is not possible to show how exactly institutional control, economic power, professional organization or journalistic routines and values work without a detailed analysis of their actual social enactment in the many activities of news production" (van Dijk, 1988a, p.98).[2] Cognitive science, then, far from being of little consequence for those interested in understanding newswork from a sociological perspective, offers important ways to explore precisely how such factors have their effects.

If that were all cognitive science had to offer, that would be considerable. But the application of recent understandings in cognitive science to the study of newswork offers much more. In fact, this knowledge identifies a range of phenomena, extending well beyond the much studied phenomenon of story selection, to describe and explain. In so doing, it offers numerous possibilities for new research on how journalists process the news.

In the pages that follow, we discuss some of the research that has been produced in recent years by cognitive scientists. Specifically, we discuss an area of cognitive psychology dealing with cognitive bias and error. This research, we believe, offers important insights into how the media construct journalistic versions of reality, and into the age-old issue of media bias.

In settling on this one particular area of cognitive science, we do not mean to suggest that it is the only area in this wide-ranging field of study that people in our field might explore. Clearly, it is not. But it is one that we believe to be especially well developed and of particular value to the study of newswork.

The structure of our monograph is straightforward. In the first section, we discuss media bias and ways in which researchers have investigated both the messages that journalists construct and the factors influencing those constructions. In addition, we introduce our argument that research on cognitive bias and error may have something valuable to contribute to such investigations. In subsequent sections, we discuss basic cognitive processes, review selected research studies with respect to these processes, and speculate as to how the cognitive biases and errors that psychologists have identified may influence the production of news. Finally, we consider some of the ramifications of this work for studies of newsmaking.

In producing this monograph, we have been provided with helpful comments and support from many people, including (but not limited to) Dan Berkowitz, Sharon Dunwoody, Dave Kennamer, Nancy La-Marca, Dave Nord, Elise Parsigian, Dave Pritchard, David Roskos-Ewoldsen, Mark Snyder, David Weaver, Ron Westrum, and the students of the first author's graduate seminar on the newsgathering process.

Five anonymous reviewers from the ranks of mass communications and psychology provided additional feedback and creative insight. Bruce Tone, of ERIC/RCS, provided World Class editing. Michael Shermis and Lauren Bongiani of ERIC, and Jan Sorby of the Graphics Department of Indiana University offered highly professional production skills. Cathi Norton and Glenda Ketcham of the

School of Journalism at Indiana University provided superb secretarial support. And many others, most especially Victoria Bedford and Bill Timberlake, offered the kind of psychological support that untenured faculty need when taking the risks that a long, speculative publication such as this entails.

To all of these people, and to the unnamed journalists who generously participated in exploratory research on this subject, we express our deep gratitude. Whatever shortcomings remain in the monograph are entirely of our own making.

As we put this monograph to rest, it is our hope, and the hope of many who have aided us in these efforts, that this document will generate interest in cognitive science on the part of investigators of newswork. If up until now we have been blind to some of the possibilities for study raised here, it may be, at least in part, because we have become captive of prevailing assumptions that prevent us from seeing them.

—*S. Holly Stocking*
—*Paget H. Gross*

Chapter I

Media Bias, Cognitive Bias?

It is a well-known fact that politicians used to snicker when Walter Cronkite ended his newscast with "That's the way it is." To many in public office at the time, the version of reality presented on CBS, as well as in other mainstream news media, did not mirror reality as they knew it. Indeed, the media distorted reality, and badly.

Charges of media distortion have not subsided since the days of Walter Cronkite, of course. Politicians on both ends of the political spectrum continue to lambast the news media for biasing news in ways they find irritating at best, destructive at worst. Nor are such allegations limited to politicians. Letters-to-the-editor from members of the general public are rife with charges of journalistic slanting. More significantly, survey research suggests that only a minority of the public thinks the news media are unbiased (Gallup, cited in Stevenson & Greene, 1980); the rest believe the media slant the news, though as with the politicians, there is considerable disagreement about the direction of slanting (pro conservatives/pro liberals).

Many social scientists who study the news likewise have concluded in recent years that the news media, rather than mirroring the "way it is," as Cronkite used to suggest, do distort. Put in a more neutral way, the news media construct reality from the "buzzing, blooming confusion" of the world; in the process, they often fail to mirror "reality" as demographers, sources, and audiences perceive it. Indeed, the question researchers of the news ask these days seems to be less *whether* news media distort than *how*? What is the particular *version* of reality that journalists construct, and even more importantly, what factors determine that construction?

Early studies of newswork stressed the role that individual reporters and editors play in shaping the news. For example, the now classic "gatekeeping" studies examined how newspaper wire editors selected news from the wire services, and found that individual news editors' values and attitudes shaped the selection of such news (see, for example, White, 1950).[3]

More recently, sociologically trained researchers, who have been the prime students of journalistic behavior, have sought explanations for journalists' versions of reality in the environments in which journalists work. Contemporary gatekeeper studies, for example, have found that the selection of wire news is less influenced by the news editor's idiosyncratic values and attitudes than it is by the configuration of news (the order and emphasis of stories, for example) that comes across the wires (McCombs & Shaw, 1976; Whitney, 1982).

Other researchers have examined the role that deadlines, space constraints, beat systems and organizational policies, characteristics of the community and culture, and a host of other environmental factors play in the construction of news (Breed, 1955; Herman & Chomsky, 1988; Crouse, 1973; Dunwoody, 1981; Epstein, 1973; Fishman, 1980; Tichenor, Donohue, & Olien, 1980; Tuchman, 1978).

In fact, so extensive has been such work that environmental factors now are seen as the critical influences in the construction of news (Shoemaker, 1987). If news is biased, it is argued, it has less to do with the individuals who process the news and more to do with the organizations, communities, and cultures within which they work (Nord, 1985). Put another way, if news is biased, it is biased primarily by factors that lie outside the control of individual reporters and editors.

It would be foolish to dismiss environmental influences on newsmaking. Environmental explanations have immense face validity, and considerable empirical support. As others have pointed out (Hirsch, 1977), they also offer a much needed antidote to the popular view that individual journalists are primarily responsible for news bias. Indeed, such explanations do much to leaven the self-determining view that many journalists hold of themselves (Hetherington, 1985; Weaver & Wilhoit, 1986), and that is regularly reflected and amplified in autobiographical and cinematic accounts of journalism (*e.g.*, the portrayal of the journalist in "Absence of Malice").

However, perhaps because of this emphasis on environmental constraints, we know very little, and certainly far less than we might, about what goes on in the minds of reporters and editors who process the news. This is not to say that investigators have ignored how journalists think; they have not (see, for example, Wearden, 1987). But studies that take the thinking of journalists as their primary emphasis remain rarities in the literature of newsmaking. Even more importantly, few such studies have been informed by an impressive body of recent research that psychologists and other cognitive scientists have developed on cognitive processing.

In the years since newsmaking became an object of systematic study by social scientists, cognitive scientists have learned a great deal about how people organize, retain, retrieve, and integrate information, and some of this research has great potential relevance to those who wish to understand better how journalists construct and thereby "bias" the news.

Cognitive scientists have documented repeatedly that the mind actively operates on external stimuli, taking incoming sensory input and processing it in memory, so that in the end, what people perceive and remember and make inferences about are not replicas of the outside world, but something quite different. Cognitive scientists thus share with recent sociologists of newswork the assumption that "reality" is actively constructed; only instead of placing the emphasis on social factors that lead to the construction, they place the emphasis on cognitive factors. They are concerned, in short, with cognitive constructions of reality.[4]

From the cognitive perspective, how the mind constructs reality is a function in part of general capacities of the brain. While researchers have not provided a precise figure on capacity, it is widely agreed that only a relatively small amount of information (some say seven plus-or-minus two chunks of information) can be attended to at any one time. Because the capacity of the human information processing system is in many ways limited, people in trying to sort and make sense of stimuli often take mental shortcuts and fall back on familiar and preferred cognitive routines. Most of the time these shortcuts and routines are highly adaptive.[5] However, sometimes in the act of processing information, people do not entertain as many perspectives (or "realities") as they might, and/or they are led to conclusions that conflict with widely shared agreements about what constitutes "reality."

Research has shown, for example, that people, even when instructed to be objective, tend to seek and select information in ways that confirm their initial beliefs. Other research has highlighted common distortions in memory, including a tendency to distort memories of an event to conform to new information about the event. Research on the way people make inferences has shown that individuals often select data from small and unreliable samples, ignore biases in existing samples, and ignore abstract statistical information about populations in favor of less reliable, but seemingly more relevant, case history or anecdotal information. Still other research has shown how people under conditions of information overload resort to stereotypical thinking.

Obviously, cognitive biases and errors encompass much more than what is usually meant by "biases" and "errors." Biases are normally thought of as the inappropriate intrusion of subjective opinion into an otherwise factual account, and errors, as incorrect facts in those accounts. Cognitive biases and errors, in contrast, consist of a variety of *ways of thinking* (indeed a variety of *routine* ways of thinking) that constrain one's perceptions and interpretations of the world.

People need not be motivationally or attitudinally biased to fall victim to cognitive biases and errors. Put another way, people do not have to have any conscious intent to bias information; nor do they have to harbor an attitude or opinion (liberal/conservative, or pro-Arab/anti-Arab) to exhibit these biases and errors (though both motivations and attitudes can affect cognitive processing, thus indirectly generating such problems). In fact, people may take active steps to be unbiased, yet still be biased, simply because of built-in constraints on the cognitive system and the attendant need to economize.

4

Although there no doubt are differences between journalists and the college student populations upon which much of this research is based, it is not unreasonable to suppose that journalists, too, systematically fall victim to these cognitive biases and errors. For example, reporters, even when they believe they are being objective, may seek and select information in ways that confirm their initial beliefs. If this is so, and if researchers can come to understand how this tendency plays itself out in a news setting, we may learn not only something of interest to those who study the news but also something of potential value to those who produce it.

Journalists, it goes without saying, are among our most visible processors of information. What they say on the air and write in their columns can set private and public agendas; under some circumstances, they can even initiate behavioral change. Given their importance for both individuals and society, it is imperative that we use all the insights at our disposal—including insights about cognitive constraints and processes—to understand better how they do their jobs.

Chapter II

Cognitive Processes in Journalism: An Overview

Reports of observers of newswork vary on the precise nature and sequence of tasks that individual journalists perform in their work.[6] However, like the lay persons studied by cognitive scientists, journalists appear regularly to perform a variety of cognitive tasks as they go about their business. These tasks include categorizing the people and events they have determined are newsworthy,[7] generating theories or hypotheses about them, selecting information to test these theories or hypotheses, and integrating the information into a coherent news story—all tasks that cognitive psychologists have studied in some depth in recent years (Hastie & Carlston, 1980; Hastie, Ostrom, Ebbesen, Wyer, Hamilton, & Carlston, 1980).

These tasks, most of which are identified in the following flowchart and summarized in this section,[8] are not exhaustive of the cognitive processes that researchers have identified, or those that are potentially identifiable.[9] However, they are ones that have been well-documented in the research literature, have received broad-based support, and seem, on the surface of it, to be among the most relevant for work in this field.

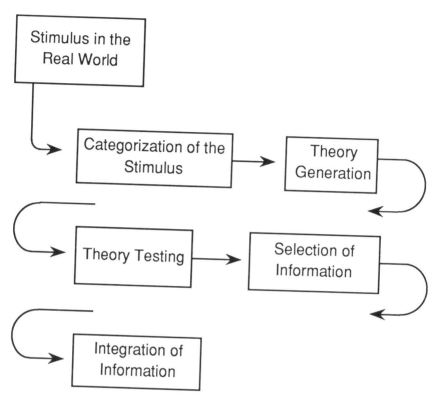

Categorization

Reporters encounter a variety of stimuli in their everyday work. These include events, such as a new scientific discovery, a murder on Tenth Street, or a military coup in a Central American country; and they include people, such as politicians, country music singers, white-collar criminals, or the survivors of a tornado or plane crash.

Such stimuli are understood by matching them with stored information that is the same as or similar to the real-world stimuli (Shank & Abelson, 1977; Leddo, Abelson, & Gross, 1984; Abelson & Lalljee, 1987). In other words, a real-world stimulus can be recognized and labeled because we have seen it before and can match the current instantiation to a stored memory of one like it. To make this obvious, perceivers need not learn about Siamese cats every time one is encountered. We understand a friend's new Siamese because we have a stored memory of others like the present one. Similarly, our ability to recognize and label new events like murders, fires, and Presidential campaigns is made possible because of the cognitive representation of events like them stored in memory.

Journalists categorize events and people all the time. They match a sudden outburst of group violence to the category *riot*, and so "understand" the disturbance as a riot. They match a widely acclaimed singer to the category *rock star* and understand the person as such.

This matching process of a real event to a stored category (categorization) seems to perceivers to occur in an almost immediate and automatic fashion. And this may be true for highly familiar and unambiguous stimuli like fires or presidential campaigns (Lalljee & Abelson, 1983; Abelson & Lalljee, 1987). Moreover, when the match to category occurs uneventfully and with a great deal of consensus, it leads us to suspect that our categorizations and labeling of events are "accurate" (or "objective" if you will).

However, the biasing influence of this matching process on the reporting of an event can be seen when events are ambiguous, or when there is the possibility of categorizing the event in different, even disparate, ways. This will be discussed more fully below, but an example drawn from recent headlines may be useful here.

American military involvement in Central American countries has been categorized and labeled by some reporters as "another Vietnam." The categorization process may lead other reporters to match the event to liberty-seeking rebellions like our own American Revolution. Having categorized the event in these different ways, all subsequent information gathering, the evaluation of further events and so on, will proceed in very different directions. Thus, categorization may be intimately tied to the course of a story.

Theory Generation

After an event is categorized, people use information within the category to guide them in the generation of theories about the event such that the event can be fully understood or described. Further, the category suggests questions to ask about the event that assist the perceiver in fleshing out this understanding or description. Thus, thinking about a Central American country as "another Vietnam" may lead to the theory that "increased military involvement in [that country] is a risky idea and likely to lead to escalation."

Theory Testing

Once a theory is in place, people engage in a process of theory testing. Among other things, they develop questions to test the accuracy of the theory. For example: What kind of military involvement is being proposed? Does the U.S. intend to send military equipment, advisers, or troops? To whom are they being sent, and to what end? Thus, categorization of involvement as another Vietnam promotes the development of a better articulated theory, which in turn generates a set of questions designed to investigate this specific possibility. Another theory may promote other questions. As we shall see, the range and type of questions asked, and even the questioning process itself, can influence the description and reporting of this event.

Selection of Information

Not only may categorization processes, theory generation, and the active testing of theories via questioning bias the production of news, but so may subsequent processes that facilitate the selection of incoming information. For example, just as people prefer to *seek* information that is consistent with their theories, they prefer to *select incoming* information that is consistent with their theories.[10] More precisely, when choosing between incoming information that is consistent with their theories and incoming information that is inconsistent, people tend to regard the supportive information as more valid. In addition, as we shall see, people tend to focus on aspects of people and events that stand out for them in some way—that is, that are salient. People may also preferentially select anecdotal information over more abstract statistical information, even if the later information is more valid and reliable.

Integration of Information

Not only must journalists select information, they must integrate information. Among other things, they must interpret the bits of information they have taken in, and piece together their causal connectedness. In determining the causes of events or others' behaviors, and in linking events together so that the events constitute a coherent story, they may fall victim to a number of cognitive biases. These include, as we shall see, a tendency to perceive relationships where none may exist, and a tendency, when explaining others' behavior, to overestimate the importance of a person's personal characteristics relative to situational factors.

In addition to identifying causes and constructing causal sequences, journalists must also recall and reconstruct information, either from memory or notes. Interestingly, recall and reconstruction may include drawing information from both the real-world event and the stored memorial event. Thus, one frequently goes beyond the information abstracted and selected from the target event and fills in any missing pieces from events like it stored in memory. This inference process is often done unintentionally, and, moreover, has certain features that can leave distortions in the construction of a new category containing the news event.

Finally, at some point in the production of news, reporters must decide when they will regard the event as fully described or the story as fully told. The decision here is one of judging when the information gathering is over. Although there is less research evidence about how this decision may be made than there is for the other subprocesses described, there are some recent studies to suggest that time pressures close off information gathering and evaluative processes, and in so doing, profoundly increase the information biases we have mentioned.

What will become evident in the description of these processes is that they are highly related and interactive. The single-line arrows from categorization to integration of information in the flowchart oversimplify the real nature of the system, but are retained in the interest of clarity. In reality, these processes interact, as many of the illustrative studies described in subsequent pages will underscore.

Chapter III

Categorization

Categorization, as already noted, is basic to human understanding of the world. It is the prior knowledge that people have about the world that allows them to organize and make sense of incoming information. As in the example given above, our understanding of Siamese cats is made possible by matching our sensory impression (the percept) to a representation stored in memory (a cognitive structure).

The influence of cognitive structures on perception goes beyond simple understanding, however. While the ordinary person regards perception as the taking in of information from the environment and creating a literal copy, research on cognitive processing provides a very different view. What is perceived is not a copy, but rather a highly constructed version of the real-world event. It is the matching of events to stored categories that creates this filtered, sometimes distorted, new construction (see Appendix).

Given the fundamental nature of categorization to understanding, categorization is the starting point from which all other processes—the labeling of the event, the generation of theories, the evaluation of information—proceed. Thus, all of the processes given in the flowchart (p. 8) are directly tied to the interaction of incoming stimuli with specific cognitive representations in memory. Categorization processes, therefore, have a directive influence on the course of the reporter's story. Two direct, perhaps the most immediate, consequences of categorization on the perception of events are *labeling* and *inference*, each of which affects *judgments*.

Labeling

Once a person or event has been categorized, things associated with the person or event are labeled in keeping with the category. Thus, once a journalist who stereotypes black people categorizes a person in a story as a "typical black," he may identify or label subsequent actions of that person in stereotypical ways.

In an illustrative study by Duncan (1976), perceivers were asked to report what they saw in a videotape of a two-party interaction. In the videotape two individuals were seen to have a dispute. One videotape showed this interaction with two white males; a second showed the identical interaction between one white and one black male.

Perceivers viewing the interaction of two whites described the physical interplay of targets as a "bump," or accidental lean, one to another. The exact same action on the part of the black was described as a "shove." Thus, perceivers filtering the latter event through a stereotype of blacks, in which aggressive behavior is one of the stored category attributes, identified the act in a way that revealed the category's influence on what was perceived. News events involving black-white interactions may be similarly biased.

However, the role of categorization on the identification or labeling of people and events may not be limited to those cases involving social stereotypes. The reporting of any ambiguous event may reveal the influence of categorization on identification and labeling (Higgins, Rholes, & Jones, 1977). Continuing the earlier example of U.S. military involvement in Central America, individuals who have categorized the event as "another Vietnam" may label a meeting between a member of the U.S. cabinet and the leader of the threatened country as "a first step toward U.S. military escalation." Similarly, a reporter who has categorized a president as a "lame duck," may identify subsequent actions taken by the president as "symptoms of a presidency in terminal decline" (DeFrank, 1987).

In all of this, it is essential to understand that events, in and of themselves, do not have meaning. They are given meaning by the perceiving individual. Because of the perceivers' active role in this process, it is possible for different perceivers to label or construct the same events in very different ways.

This is not to say that people always construct the same events in different ways. Obviously, there can be universal (or near-universal) agreement on the construction of some events (*e.g.*, "this is a fire").

It is also true that groups of people can share the same "reality." Indeed, as Gans (1980) has pointed out in his discussion of journalists' values, and as critical scholars have noted in discussions of ideology and the news (see, for example, Gitlin, 1980), a group of journalists may share a world view. Or they may share more specific perceptions about people and events, as when reporters and editors share stereotypes about a group of people.

Journalists and their *sources* may also construct people and events in similar ways.[11] Similarities in construction seem, in fact, to be common-place in journalism, where journalists often take their cues from bureau-cracies (Fishman, 1980; Tuchman, 1978) and from other journalists and news media (Dunwoody, 1981; Crouse, 1973).

Donohue, Tichenor, and Olien (1989), for example, have pointed out that journalists covering a powerline controversy in Minnesota acted as "agents of legitimacy within the system," constructing events in ways that often mirrored the constructions of those in power. More precisely, journalists labeled environmental activity as "protest" so long as there was considerable statewide support for the protest groups; however, once the power lines were built, and it was obvious that protesters were waging a losing battle, they labeled the protests as "vandalism," which, as Donohue *et al.* note, "was a major delegitimizing reference." From a contemporary cognitive perspective, then, much status quo reporting might be understood as resulting from journalists' reliance on others' categorizations and from subsequent labeling of people and events. The same might be said for "pack" journalism, in which journalists, working together and using the same news sources, pursue *en masse* the same story (Crouse, 1973).

Inference

A second direct consequence of categorization is an inference process that serves to fill in aspects of the event which are not immediately taken in or even present. In inference, one essentially goes beyond the given data, fleshing out the skeletal picture, with information from the stored category representation (Bransford & Franks, 1971; Cantor & Mischel, 1977). Thus, an event described by an observer may contain, in part, aspects of the current event, and in part information from the schema that is consistent with the event, but that never actually appeared.

Consider the following example adapted from Bower, Black, and Turner, 1979; Bransford and Franks, 1971; Graesser, Woll, Kowalski, and Smith, 1980; and Smith and Graesser, 1981. People are asked to observe a woman who has entered a restaurant. The woman is seated by a hostess. She orders food, pays her bill, and leaves. The sequences of events that typically occur in restaurants are commonly known and considered to form a script, a category containing knowledge about events, the unfolding of which most people could describe with ease. Interestingly, if one asks people to report what they have seen, their reports will include events that are drawn from the stored cognitive script, but which are actually not given in the experience. People may report that a waiter brought the woman her food, when this, in fact, was never observed.

In 1968, Lindsy Van Gelder of the *New York Post* covered the early feminist demonstrations at the Miss America pageant in Atlantic City. At the time, anti-Vietnam demonstrators were burning draft cards to protest the war. Although historians of the women's movement have ascertained that bras, girdles, and curlers were never burned at Atlantic City (they were thrown into a wastebasket; see Tuchman, 1978, p.138), Van Gelder wrote a light, witty story reporting that they were. To be sure, there are many ways to interpret what happened,[12] and we may never know what happened with certainty; but it is highly plausible, given a cognitive perspective, that Van Gelder, who has said she was aware that other demonstrators (those against the Vietnam War) were burning draft cards at the time, linked the feminist demonstrators and their actions with the Vietnam demonstrators and the "demonstration script" provided by the latter. Eager to get the story in the paper and with draft-card burning in mind, Van Gelder (and/or her sources) may have "inferred" bra-burning where none existed.

Judgment

Not only do people use information from stored categories to flesh out their sensory impression of events but also they use these fleshed-out versions of events to make subsequent judgments. Indeed, investigators have discovered that sometimes people rely more on the elaborated version of the event than on the original percept when making subsequent judgments (Wyer & Gordon, 1982).

This is nicely demonstrated in a study by Gilovich (1981) in which subjects were asked to make recommendations about how to resolve a hypothetical international crisis. The crisis situation, in which a democratic nation was threatened by its totalitarian neighbor, was presented along with minimal information to suggest historical analogies to the war in Vietnam or American intervention in pre-World War II Europe.

Two outcomes of the study are important. First, subjects used the historical analogies to add to the presented description of the crisis situation, and second, subjects made judgments about an appropriate course of action that was consistent with those categorizations and elaborations. Subjects who constructed the situation as like that of pre-WW II Europe made stronger recommendations for interventionist strategies than did those constructing the event as "another Vietnam."

To continue an example used earlier, if reporters construct the U.S.'s involvement in the affairs of a Central American country as "another Vietnam," we might expect recommendations and judgments about courses of action, provided implicitly in news reports or explicitly in editorials, to reveal the influence of this category-based construction.

Chapter IV

Theory Generation

Journalists, it can be argued, not only categorize people and events but also seem to develop more complex theories about them, and gather information to test these theories. Indeed, in the views of many observers of the news (see, for example, Mencher, 1987, and Franklin, 1987), journalists regularly pursue hypotheses.

Occasionally, this pursuit is a very conscious phenomenon. For instance, in their book *Raising Hell: How the Center for Investigative Reporting Gets the Story*, investigative reporters David Weir and Dan Noyes include in their list of investigative techniques what they call the "investigative hypothesis." The investigative hypothesis, they write, "gives shape and direction to a budding investigation. The theory should be grounded in fact and experience and take the story beyond what is presently known to what seems a likelihood" (Weir & Noyes, 1983, p. 315).

More often, the reporter simply goes after an "idea." Bill Blundell, writing coach for the *Wall Street Journal*, encourages reporters to "identify in advance potential action elements in the story—the moves and countermoves that have high reader interest" (Blundell, 1986, p. 23; 1988, p. 24). If there is a nationwide shortage of physicians, for instance, Blundell urges reporters to speculate about the effects of the shortage as a way to narrow the story. One effect of a doctor shortage may be inferior medical care; this, in turn, may lead to angry patients, lawsuits, and higher malpractice fees. Another effect may be overworked and stressed physicians, which may in turn lead to more use of drugs and alcohol, more suicides, more family problems, more doctors quitting or limiting their practice. Any one of these potential "effects" could make a single story.

Although Blundell never uses the term *theory* or *hypothesis* when he helps journalists shape their stories in this way, he is clearly encouraging them to generate hypotheses or theories, which they will subsequently test.

Thus, although we have little systematic data on this matter, it would seem that journalists are "in an important sense hypothesis testers, whose newsgathering procedures consist of checking the empirical validity of their preconceptions" (Sigelman, 1973, pp.144-145). So a journalist may theorize that the presidency is in decline, and generate questions to investigate this hypothesis. Similarly, a reporter may theorize that outpatient programs for the mentally ill contribute to the problem of homelessness, and generate questions to investigate this theory.

Content of Theories

Journalists' theories (or hypotheses) appear to be about many things. Reporters may speculate about the character of a political candidate. They may theorize about the cause of a chemical spill, the reason a killer went berserk, why a favorite coach is leaving for another coaching position, or the explanations for a high infant mortality rate. They may speculate about the consequences of a bottle tampering incident on people and sales, the results of a statewide campaign against smoking, the impact of a sculptor on the world of art, or the consequences of the new baby boomlet for the fashion industry. They may theorize that there's a decline in celebrity charity events, or a blood shortage in the state.

In short, they may theorize about a person's character, about the causes and consequences of events, behavior, and phenomena, about changes in phenomena, or even about the existence of phenomena. Writing coach Blundell seems to have recognized many of these facts. In an in-house manual for *Journal* reporters, he has identified some of the routine concerns of reporters writing profiles and covering trends or developments. For developments, these include the scope of the phenomenon, its causes, its impacts, and countermoves taken against it. For profiles, these include (but are not limited to) the person's values and effects on others (Blundell, 1986; 1988). In addition to theorizing about such concerns, it would appear that journalists also harbor simple expectancies about people or events. For example, reporters may expect the victims of homelessness to be unkempt and unpredictable in social contexts. They may predict that a particular speaker before the city council will have nothing of value to say. Or, they may speculate that America will continue to escalate its involvement in a Central American country, just as it did in Vietnam.

Variations in Complexity and Stability

Not only does it appear that journalists' theories are about many things but also they appear to range in terms of complexity. Journalists' theories may be simple. They may be complex and elaborate. Or journalists may entertain both, depending on what is being reported upon, and on the journalists' stored representations of it.

In producing a single story, a reporter may entertain one overriding theory, referred to by journalists as a "theme" or "focus," and multiple sub-theories. So, for example, in entertaining the possibility of a citywide crime wave, a reporter may entertain many related possibilities—that violent crimes are increasing faster than nonviolent crimes, that crime prevention programs are failing for lack of funding, and/or that a rise in unemployment is contributing to the problem.

Theory generation is quite clearly tied to the way in which an event is categorized. Sometimes, as we shall see, the evocation of theories can happen so automatically that it may seem as if categorization and theory generation are one and the same. Thus, pursuing the theory that the presidency is in decline is closely linked to the categorization of the president as a "lame duck." And pursuing the theory that out-patient-care programs for the mentally ill contribute to the problem of homelessness is closely tied to the categorization of the homeless as "mentally ill."

The generation of theories may arise from categorization processes that are stable and enduring, or those that are more momentary and transient. For example, a reporter who typically covers human interest stories may consistently categorize people in relational terms (husbands, wives, lovers, in-laws) and theorize about subjects in terms of personal or intimate components, while a reporter who typically covers the world scene may consistently categorize events in terms of political ideologies and historical conflicts and generate theories that encompass the broader implications of events for global affairs.

So, a reporter who regularly writes "people" stories may theorize about hunger and poverty from the perspective of the individual (hunger and poverty numb the soul), giving little attention to the social and economic causes of hunger and poverty. The reporter who writes more consistently from a social and economic perspective, on the other hand, may generate theories that are more "macro" or "structural" in nature (the causes of the current hunger crisis are embedded in our social, political, or economic system).

Some theories, as noted, have a more transient nature. They may be evoked by a current event or by something the reporter has just read or used in an immediate context, and then they may drop away. The process whereby a momentarily salient theory (or category) is immediately evoked is referred to in social cognition literature as "priming" (Higgins, Rholes, & Jones, 1977; Higgins, King, & Mavin, 1982).

As an example of priming, consider the reporter who has just finished reading a book on the training of medical doctors. Among other things, the book discusses the number of mistakes that are made in July and August as new medical interns begin their rounds in major teaching hospitals. Primed to think about such mistakes, the reporter theorizes that an apparent increase in deaths at his city's teaching hospital in July may be due to a new round of interns.

Or take the reporter who has recently seen a made-for-TV movie about an accident in a nuclear weapons manufacturing plant; primed to think about the possibility for accidents at nuclear power plants, he theorizes about the possibility for such accidents in a nearby weapons factory. Likewise, the reporter who has received releases from anti-vivisectionist groups about the inhumane treatment of animals in research labs theorizes that animals at his local university are not getting the kind of care they ought to receive under university regulations and federal law.

Expert-Novice Differences

Theories may arise spontaneously, through a process of automatic activation, or they may be generated after deliberation or consideration of an event. Consider two reporters who are assigned to cover the launching of the space shuttle. When the shuttle tragically explodes, one reporter automatically guesses that the explosion was the result of a fluky technical glitch. The other, with greater deliberation, speculates that inadequate bureaucratic safeguards may have prompted the disaster. The decision to pursue one theory as opposed to the other may be made immediately and "automatically," in a manner that is not under the cognitive control of the perceiver (Fazio, 1986; Shiffrin & Schneider, 1977; Schneider & Schiffrin, 1977); alternatively, it may be made by deliberate decision.

There is evidence to suggest that familiarity with an event increases the tendency for theories about the event to be automatically activated (Fazio, Powell, & Herr, 1983; Fiske & Pavelchak, 1986). So, experts are more likely than novices to draw on spontaneously and continue to use well-entrenched theories that prevent them from seeing current events in new or different ways, even when this may be warranted (Fiske & Kinder, 1981; Chi & Glaser, 1979; Larkin, McDermott, Simon, & Simon, 1980).

If we take specialty journalists to be "experts" and general assignment reporters to be "novices," we thus would expect specialty reporters to be less able than those on general assignment to see the people and events they cover in needed new lights. Veteran reporters, likewise, would be expected to draw on and use more entrenched theories than beginning reporters, creating "generic brand" interpretations of people and events when fresher interpretations might offer more insight.

Such speculations are hardly new to longtime observers of newswork. Beat reporters, for example, have often been "scooped" by general assignment reporters, and for many of the reasons researchers suggest. In fact, it has long been argued that the reason *Washington Post* police reporters Bob Woodward and Carl Bernstein were able to break the Watergate story was because they did not see things in the same way as those on the White House beat. Perhaps they did not "see" things in the same way precisely because they pursued different theories about what was going on.

The theories of expert reporters may differ from those of novices in yet another way. Not surprisingly, researchers have found that familiarity or expertise is frequently associated with richer, more complex theories (Linville & Jones, 1980; Fiske & Kinder, 1981). This means, of course, that lack of familiarity, or novice status, tends to be associated with leaner, simpler theories. Given these findings, we would expect journalists lacking in expertise to have less involved theories than journalists who know the subject well. Thus, the novice reporter should be less able than the expert to consider the potential effects of a new tax law. So too the general assignment reporter should be less able than the business reporter to speculate as to the varied causes of a new banking regulation.

If such speculations appear obvious, others may be less so. For example, researchers have found that experts display a greater tendency than novices to notice, recall, and use discrepant information (Fiske, Kinder, & Larter, 1983). This suggests that novice journalists may be less likely than experienced journalists to notice, recall, and use discrepant information in their theorizing. If this is so, we might expect the journalist who rarely covers a particular health hazard to be less likely than the reporter who regularly covers the hazard to notice, recall, and use information that counters the prevailing view that the hazard will do harm. By contrast, we might expect the experienced reporter to be more likely than the novice to reason that while some populations could show adverse effects, others may not; this does not negate the prevailing view—that the hazard is harmful; it simply suggests that it may be harmful for some and not for others.

In a related vein, there is evidence that theoretical complexity moderates judgment (Fiske & Taylor, 1984). This suggests that journalists who are well-acquainted with a subject (and have incorporated a lot of inconsistent information into their theories) will generate theories that are considerably less extreme in their judgments than will journalists who know little. Conversely, journalists who are unfamiliar with a topic (and have little inconsistent information in their theories) should come up with theories that are more extreme in their judgments. So we might expect reporters who rarely cover solid waste issues to hypothesize more extreme consequences from solid waste incineration than do reporters who, as a result of regularly covering such issues, have a more complex understanding of the potential effects.

Chapter V

Theory Testing

Once a theory is in place, people set about testing the accuracy of that theory. There are two facets of the theory-testing process that are particularly relevant to news reporting.

One Theory at a Time

First, perceivers have a pervasive tendency to test one theory at a time (Wason & Johnson-Laird, 1965). That is, theories are tested sequentially, not in parallel fashion. For example, if one is testing a theory about the negative impact of feminism on women's lives, one is unlikely also to test theories about its positive impact. Similarly, if one is testing the hypothesis that a documented rise in birth defects is the result of a prior nuclear reactor accident, one may not pursue the possibility that it is *not* the result of the accident; indeed it may not even occur to the reporter that other causes—including a general increase in the birthrate—could be responsible (Stocking, 1989a).

Confirmation Bias

Second, people show a dramatic tendency to test theories using a theory-confirming strategy. That is, people have a bias toward seeking out evidence that confirms (rather than disconfirms) the theory they currently hold.[13]

There are a number of mechanisms that may operate in the service of a theory-confirming strategy, and contribute to the biased confirmation of theories. For one thing, people may preferentially select sources who are likely to confirm rather than disconfirm their theories. Second, they may limit the scope or type of questions they ask—preferentially posing those that will elicit information that supports their hypotheses. Third, and not unrelated, they may handle sources in such a way (coddling or harassing, for example) that they elicit behavior that confirms their hypotheses. Finally, they may draw theory-confirming inferences from questions unanswered or denied by a person, using the question itself, not the answer, as evidence. Each of these mechanisms of theory confirmation is described below.

Sourcing. Although to date psychologists have not had much to say on the matter, the tendency of individuals to seek theory-confirming evidence is so strong—occurring even when one is instructed to be unbiased—that it is not unreasonable to suppose that reporters may adopt theory-confirming strategies when they select their sources. That is, reporters may quite unconsciously seek out sources whose answers will confirm their theories. So, reporters entertaining the theory that a leak of radiation from a nuclear reactor is responsible for a documented increase in birth defects might not seek sources who question this hypothesis. Instead, they might go to a local academic with expertise on the effects of radiation on developing fetuses (Stocking, 1989a).

Such biased information seeking may begin the moment a reporter decides to do a story. Fishman (1980) has noticed, for example, that some reporters' search process is improvised and idiosyncratic—the reporter looks to a book just read to provide perspective, or asks a friend whom he thinks might know someone. In a related vein, Elliott (1972) has shown that a television production team, guided by their own preconceptions about the documentary they were producing, sought out personal contacts that would help them to realize their ideas. Thus, it would appear that which sources are consulted may depend a great deal on the theories one is entertaining.

Not only may journalists sample sources in a biased way but also they may ignore the fact that there are inherent inaccuracies associated with the drawing of conclusions from existing biased samples. Here we may include samples of data that have been provided by one source or another, such as the data provided by one lobby group, one group within the medical community, or one media source. Psychologists have found people to be insufficiently attentive to the characteristics of samples, including who was sampled or the method of sampling—features that would inform them about the generalizability of the sample to the larger population (Tversky & Kahneman, 1974; Nisbett & Ross, 1980).

Wilhoit and Weaver (1980) have pointed out this problem in journalists' use of poll data. But the problem shows up in other ways as well. For example, Tankard (1976, pp. 51-52) points to the way journalists covered the Watergate hearings during the 1970s. One reporter, using letters reportedly sent to Senator Ervin's committee, concluded that televised hearings were appreciated by audiences, while another reporter, judging from call-ins to television personnel who had pre-empted sports programming to televise the hearings, concluded just the opposite. Apparently, neither reporter stopped to consider the inherent biases of the samples used in drawing their conclusions.

Questioning. Once people have decided with whom to talk, they may preferentially ask questions of these sources that solicit confirming rather than disconfirming evidence. In one of the earliest studies on theory-confirming bias in information gathering, Snyder and Swann (1978) provided subjects with either a thumbnail description of a prototypic introvert (shy, uncomfortable in crowds) or a prototypic extravert (gregarious and sociable). Subjects were then told that they would have the opportunity to interact with a person whom they had never met. Prior to the interaction, subjects were allowed to select a set of questions that they would like to ask of this person in order to fulfill their task of getting to know the person better.

Subjects who had been given the description of an introvert, although having no reason to believe that this new person was indeed introverted, tested the theory that the stranger was an introvert, and did so by selecting questions that would specifically reveal aspects of the person's introverted nature. The extravert theorizers selected only questions specifically formulated to reveal the person's extraverted nature.

In addition, this hypothesis-confirming strategy so constrained the scope and type of information that the person could report back to the questioner, that perceivers with disparate sets of questions were given answers confirming of their original hypothesis about the person. Moreover, both sets of questioners regarded their hypothesis about the person as confirmed by the target's responses, and neither group thought asking additional questions was necessary. (See also Snyder & Cantor, 1979).

Subsequent research has stressed the fact that most of the questions Snyder and his colleagues used in their studies were what survey researchers would call "leading" questions (Trope & Bassok, 1982). That is, they were questions—such as "What things do you dislike about loud parties?"—that solicited confirmatory evidence without soliciting disconfirmatory evidence. Thus, it is not surprising that subjects who selected these questions obtained information that confirmed their hypotheses.

In similar experimental tasks, when subjects have been given free rein to develop their own questions, they have tended to ask more nondirectional or "diagnostic" questions. That is, they have tended to ask questions that would solicit the kind of information they need to diagnose between one hypothesis and a competing hypothesis (Trope & Bassok, 1982). For example, "Do you like loud parties?"[14]

The extent to which journalists might employ hypothesis-confirming strategies in their questioning is unclear. On the one hand, journalists may receive more training in questioning techniques than do lay perceivers, and so may be even less likely than experimental subjects to use leading questions and more likely to use nondirectional or diagnostic questions.

On the other hand, journalists work under pressures that have not been placed on subjects in the studies mentioned. For example, in the lab studies, subjects have no particular vested interest in either the "extravert" or "introvert" hypotheses, whereas that may not be the case for the journalist entertaining hypotheses related to stories. Indeed, in journalism it is not infrequently the case that one hypothesis ("X may be a liar") clearly makes for a better story than a competing hypothesis ("X may be honest"). Under such circumstances, reporters may be subtly influenced to ask the kinds of questions that will elicit the better story.

Also, in some circumstances—as when entertaining notions that appear to be widely accepted—reporters may not even be aware of competing possibilities.[15] Such circumstances are noticeably different from the extravert-introvert situations of the labs, where one hypothesis (extravert) clearly or by implication has a competing hypothesis (introvert). When unaware of competing hypotheses, journalists may unwittingly develop a range of questions that lead their sources to confirm the one notion (and no others). More precisely, journalists may ask questions of their sources that reveal only a limited sample of information.

For instance, if there is perceived to be widespread agreement (in the newsroom, in other newspapers, among sources) that there is a "crime wave" against the elderly, reporters may ask questions such as "What kinds of crimes have contributed most to the crime wave against the elderly?" or "What impact will the increased rate of crimes against the elderly have on funding for the city's crime prevention program?"

Similarly, if there appears to be widespread agreement (or wish) that devastating handicaps can be overcome, and if reporters entertain this idea without recognizing it as just one among several, they may ask questions of handicapped persons that reveal only those ways in which the disabled have managed to "master" their problems. ("How did you overcome the obstacles?")

Handling of Sources. In addition to asking questions that elicit theory-confirming information from sources, journalists may do other things in their handling of sources to elicit theory-confirming evidence. That is, guided by their beliefs about story subjects (*e.g.*, the political candidate is a "wimp" or a "bungler," or the homeless person is "mentally ill"), reporters may treat sources in ways that draw out the kind of behavior that validates these beliefs.

A number of studies have demonstrated this kind of self-fulfilling prophecy. In one well-known investigation by Snyder, Tanke, and Bersheid (1977), college-aged men were paired with college-aged women for a "get-acquainted" telephone conversation. Prior to the conversation, the men were provided with snapshots that created expectations about the attractiveness of their telephone partners. More precisely, half the men were given snapshots that led them to believe their female partners would be attractive, while the other half were given snapshots that led them to think their partner would be unattractive.

As expected, the men's beliefs led them to structure the conversation in such a way that they elicited behavior that confirmed their beliefs. To be exact, men who believed they were talking with attractive women expected them to be more poised and socially adept and so treated them with more friendliness and warmth than did men who believed they were talking with unattractive women. Moreover, as a result of the men's behavior, the women (who were not necessarily attractive and were unaware that the men had been told anything about them) acted in ways that confirmed the men's beliefs. That is, those women believed to be attractive responded to the warmth and friendliness of the men and behaved in kind; in distinct contrast, those women believed to be unattractive became cool and aloof.

One possible example of this kind of behavioral confirmation in journalism is provided in the book *Fair Play* by Burton Benjamin, former vice-president and director of CBS News (Benjamin, 1988). In the book, Benjamin offers a fascinating and fair-minded account of the making of "The Uncounted Enemy: A Vietnam Deception," the CBS documentary that led to a $120-million lawsuit by General William Westmoreland.

Among other things, Benjamin provides evidence that the journalists handled sources differentially—the many sources who were friendly to the documentary's thesis being rehearsed and "coddled" during the interviews, whereas the lesser number of sources whose views went counter to the thesis were treated noticeably more harshly. Indeed, under stern questioning from correspondent Mike Wallace, General Westmoreland, who was the villain of the piece, sweated and licked his lips. Some of the general's sweating and lip-licking may have been due to the hot lights. However, he was also put on the defensive by a line of questioning and a tone of questioning that implied he was a liar; and that defensiveness was captured on film, in tight camera close-ups. At the end of the interview, Westmoreland reportedly stormed out of the studio, saying he had been "rattlesnaked" (Benjamin, 1988, p.57).

Responding to the Raised Question. As we have seen, then, individuals may unconsciously confirm their theories by using a restricted range of sources with limited perspectives, by asking a set of questions of sources that are overly limited in scope and type, or by handling sources in ways that elicit theory-confirming evidence. Researchers have also found that individuals may draw theory-confirming inferences from questions asked, even when the target does not answer at all, or when the responses deny the validity of the questioner's theory.

Swann, Guilano, and Wegner (1982) conducted a study in which an individual was asked a series of questions all designed to reveal specific personality traits (a series of questions designed to reveal an extraverted nature, *i.e.*, "What would you do to liven up a party?") Observers of this interview were aware of two features of the situation: first, there were no real grounds for the interviewer to assume the individual questioned was extraverted by nature, and second, the responses of the questioned party cast doubt on the assumption that extraversion was an aspect of their character. Nonetheless—and perhaps because of the simple fact that the question had been raised—observers inferred that the individual must indeed be an extraverted character. Their rationale? There must have been evidence of extraversion in the character of the person or else why would the interviewer have asked the question in the first place?

The press contains numerous examples of cases in which journalists, in response to questions or charges by others, appear to have drawn theory-confirming inferences, in spite of sources' refusals to answer questions or outright denials of charges. For example, the press frequently carries news articles in which reporters entertain the possibility that a source has engaged in wrongdoing (or has known about others' wrongful activities), then note, in a sentence or two, that the source has denied the suggestion. Consider the hypothetical case in which the journalist entertains the possibility that a leading government official knew of his subordinates' misdeeds: "(The accused) conferred with his lieutenants on a regular basis. Because of this, many have argued he must have known about their dealings. However, when asked if he knew about their activities, (the accused) denied the charges."

The press also makes inferences about the future decisions of public figures in the face of outright denials. Sometimes these inferences are well-founded. In 1987, for example, a *Newsweek* reporter wrote that then

Transportation Secretary Elizabeth Dole was taking certain actions in anticipation of leaving her post to campaign for the presidency with her husband, Robert Dole. Although the article quoted Secretary Dole as denying she would be leaving, the thrust of the article from start to finish was that she would be ("Dole in fast track," 1987).

Sometimes, though, such inferences are not well-founded. Consider the case of Ginny Foat, former president of the California chapter of the National Organization for Women. In a 1983 *Time* magazine cover story on journalism, Foat was quoted as saying that from the moment she was arrested for a murder that had happened years before, the press wrote about her as though she were guilty. Reporters probed into her background, searching for evidence of character that might be consistent with the type of person who would commit a heinous crime. "They believed what a lot of people believe, that if you are arrested, you must be guilty" (Henry, 1983, p.83). Foat was acquitted after less than two hours of jury deliberation, but the press' apparent initial inferences about her, as reflected in its treatment of her case, left a mark that she is unlikely soon to forget.

As suggested by Swann's study, then, reporters may unwittingly influence their readers' judgments of a source's character or plans by simply raising questions about them, regardless of the source's response. Calvin Trillin, in a *New Yorker* profile of *Miami Herald* police reporter Edna Buchanan, seems to have recognized this fact, noting that "It could be libelous for a newspaper to call someone a suspect, but the paper can get the same idea across by quoting his denial of guilt" (Trillin, 1986, p. 40).[16]

Chapter VI

Selection of Information

Perhaps not surprisingly, given the pervasive tendency for people actively to *seek* evidence that confirms their theories, people also tend preferentially to *select incoming* information that supports their theories.

In addition, people reveal other cognitive preferences when they select information. For example, they tend to focus on aspects of people and events that stand out for them in some way—that is, that are salient. They also preferentially select anecdotal information over more abstract statistical information, even if the latter information is more valid and reliable.

Such preferences for certain kinds of information appear to exist across tasks and domains (Nisbett & Ross, 1980). Given this, there is reason to believe that these and other biases associated with the selection of incoming information, like biases in categorization, theory generation, and theory testing, may find their way into newsmaking.

Preference for Theory-Consistent Information

The tendency for people preferentially to select information that supports their theories is demonstrated in several studies that prompted perceivers to generate or adopt theories about events, and then provided them with an array of information, some of it confirming and some disconfirming of the theory. In one such study by Lord, Ross, and Lepper (1979), people who held theories about capital punishment (regarding it as either an effective or ineffective deterrent of crime) were subsequently provided with two empirical studies. One of the studies supported the deterrent effect and one did not. Regardless of the theory held, perceivers regarded the study that supported their theory as more relevant and more credible.

Similar results have been found in studies dealing with theories about children's academic abilities (Darley & Gross, 1983), personality characteristics (Swann & Snyder, 1980), political events (Fiske & Kinder, 1981), and a range of ordinary social issues (Fiske & Kinder, 1981; Judd & Kulik, 1980; Anderson, 1983).

How does one maintain a preference for theory-consistent evidence in the face of disconfirming pieces of data? There appear to be several processes that accomplish this.

First, disconfirming evidence is frequently regarded as arising from poor or shoddy sources (Lord, Ross, & Lepper, 1979). Thus, one may be particularly critical of the methodology of a disconfirming study, and in fact, so critical that the study may be discarded as entirely unreliable.

Reporters may similarly discard sources (persons or resources for data) that are disconfirming of their theories by virtue of the judged unreliability of the sources. Indeed, Fishman, in his account of how a series of events in New York City came to be linked together as a "crime wave," reports that "a week and a half after the coverage started, the police wire was steadily supplying the press with fresh incidents almost every day" (Fishman, 1980, p.10). Even when a reporter examined police crime statistics and discovered that crimes against the elderly had actually decreased (*not* increased) compared to the previous year, the crime wave theme remained in place. As Fishman tells it, "The reporter was puzzled and eventually decided to ignore the police figures. He felt they were unreliable and incomplete, and anyway he had to do the story as originally planned because the whole issue was too big to pass up or play down" (Fishman, 1980, p.5).

A second process employed to reduce the impact of disconfirmations is to regard disconfirming evidence as transient or situationally induced. As an example, a political figure who is thought to be honest and forthright and who is then caught in lies about events can be reported as being momentarily confused, or without recall, or perhaps induced to perform dishonestly by misguided advisers, or the pressure of office

(Ross, Lepper & Hubbard, 1975; Hayden & Mischel, 1976). Even if journalists themselves do not discuss actions in this way, they may regard such interpretations by others as more credible than other interpretations, and so give them more prominent play.

Yet another process employed to reduce the impact of disconfirming evidence is to regard such evidence as "superficial" and not really indicative of what is going on "underneath." Thus, if a person regarded as "self-serving" suddenly acts in a charitable manner, the charitable acts may be discounted as not indicative of true character; indeed, they may be interpreted as actions taken for self-serving motives (Hayden & Mischel, 1976).

This phenomenon can be seen in a 1987 *Wall Street Journal* article on Ivan Boesky, who, not long before the article appeared, pleaded guilty to a felony charge in Wall Street's insider trading scandal (Miller, 1987, p. 12). Throughout the article, Boesky is cast as a greedy crook; in fact, at one point, he is indirectly likened to Jack the Ripper. In explaining what Boesky had been doing with his time since he had become involved in the scandal, the *Journal* reporter noted that, among other things, he was looking for a volunteer job. This was something, the reporter added, that *"a lot of white-collar crooks do to impress sentencing judges"* (italics added).

Research suggests that such discounting mechanisms may be especially likely when a theory is easily accessible (Houston & Fazio, 1989). So we might expect a journalist whose elderly relative has been mugged, and so has a strong (and presumably more accessible) belief that crimes against the elderly are on the increase, to be especially likely to discount police statistics that show a downturn in such crimes.

Whether these discounting mechanisms lead to correct or incorrect conclusions, they are employed quite sincerely. People regard consistent information as eminently true and reliable such that counters to that information seem to perceivers to require an accounting or explaining away. Indeed, one odd effect of encountering inconsistent evidence is that it can sometimes prompt perceivers to think about the inconsistency, explain it away, and become even more sure that their original hypothesis was the most correct and tenable (Hastie & Kumar, 1979). As a result, after finding evidence to disconfirm a theory, a polarization may result that strengthens, not weakens, the theory (Lord, Ross & Lepper, 1979).

In the observation of ongoing activity, people show a similar selectivity for theory-confirming evidence. The mechanism that produces this effect is not clearly understood; however, unlike some other theory-confirming biases where perceivers may sometimes be able to make deliberate choices, it is not generally regarded as a controlled or thoughtful process (Darley & Gross, 1983; Fazio & Herr, 1984).

Thus, if we regard a politician as deceitful, we are likely to confirm this while observing his ongoing behavior, perhaps taking note of his shifting glance or shaking hands. Evidence of his stalwart stance, which may serve to disconfirm our theory, may go unnoticed. *Washington Post* reporters Bernstein and Woodward (1974) provide what appears to be a good example of this phenomenon when discussing their attendance at a presidential news conference some time after they had begun to publish disclosures concerning White House connections to the Watergate break-in. While observing the press conference, they noticed that Nixon's hands shook throughout the session. Toward the end of the story that they subsequently wrote on the press conference, they included this detail. Other reporters, who had not been as close to the Watergate story as Woodward and Bernstein, did not describe Nixon's shaking hands, though they did later confirm the accuracy of the observation.[17]

If Woodward and Bernstein paid attention to Nixon's hands, while other reporters did not, it may have been because they, unlike other reporters, were operating under the strong assumption that Nixon was guilty of wrongdoing, and this bit of information simply supported that assumption. In any event, the shaking hands were subsequently edited out by the *Post*'s editors.

As another example, sports reporters may focus selectively on the "dirty" plays of the opposing team, which they believe plays "dirty" as a matter of routine, and may give little attention to comparably "dirty" tactics on the part of the home team. Hastorf and Cantrill (1954), found evidence for just such differential perception/attention in student coverage of a particularly "dirty" game between Princeton and Dartmouth in 1951 (cited in Loftus, 1979, p.40). Similarly, war correspondents may focus selectively on enemy atrocities or violations of treaties, while similar atrocities on the part of Americans do not attract attention. Thus, the unevenness of attention may result in the unevenness of perception and reporting of the entire scene.

Saliency Biases. While consistency biases depend on cues from the perceiver's *a priori* theories, other biases may depend on cues from the environment. One of the most important of these stimulus cues is the saliency of a person or event in the environment. Perceivers show a strong bias to focus on stimuli that are salient. The saliency of a person or event is determined relative to the broader context in which that person or event is located.

Fiske and Taylor (1984) have identified three general classes of contextual saliency. People or events that are perceptually figural (which stand out, like an explosion, because they are bright, moving, or complex) may grab attention; so may people or events that are novel (first or only woman, black, Hispanic, etc.) relative to other people or events. People or events that appear unusual or unexpected (an event that does not unfold as planned, for example, or negative or extreme behavior) may be attention-grabbing. Finally, a person or event relevant to the reporter's goals may arrest attention.

Saliency can be expected to affect reporting by attracting attention to some features of a person or event and detracting attention from other features. A police reporter, for example, may look for those aspects of a murder that cause her to say "That's interesting as heck" (Trillin, 1986), and pay less attention to those aspects that are humdrum but could reveal trends and the underlying causes of murders in a town.

Likewise, a reporter covering this year's Nobel Prize winners may pay attention to those factors that appear to be unexpected in a winner (she looks like a "Bronx housewife") and less attention to those factors that are usual, but perhaps more important (the scientists' qualifications and research). Sociologist Dorothy Nelkin, in a book on media coverage of science and technology, offers examples that suggest just such a proclivity on the part of reporters covering Nobel Prize winners. For example, in an article about Rosalyn Yalow, winner of the 1977 Nobel Prize in medicine, a reporter for *Family Health* magazine wrote that she had expected to meet "a crisp, efficient, no nonsense type," but discovered instead that Yalow "looked as though she would be at home selling brownies for the PTA fund raiser" (cited in Nelkin, 1987, p.19).

In addition to drawing attention, saliency has one other potent effect. People are more likely to make extreme judgments about salient stimuli. To illustrate, in a study conducted by Taylor (1981), a solo woman or a solo black was seen interacting in a group of white males. The solo target was regarded by those watching the interaction as having a greater impact on the discussion and was the recipient of more extreme reactions. In an identical context in which the black was joined by other blacks and was no longer a highly salient person, his same comments were evaluated less extremely and seen as having considerably less impact on the discussion.

It is not hard to find examples in the press of extreme judgments toward salient people. Consider Geraldine Ferraro, the first female vice-presidential candidate on a major ticket. The press, in covering her candidacy, subjected her to a scrutiny, with attendant judgments, that many have regarded as extreme. Or consider Jesse Jackson, the only black candidate in the presidential races of 1984 and 1988. Jackson certainly seemed to think he was the recipient of extreme press reactions, remarking during the 1984 campaign that if it were discovered that he could walk on water, the press version of the story would read, "Jackson can't swim."[18]

Anecdotal versus Base-Rate Information. In the reporting of many social and political issues, journalists may be presented with two kinds of evidence that describe the phenomena at hand—statistical estimates (prior probabilities or proportions) or specific concrete examples. In reporting about welfare abuse, for example, journalists may be presented with statistical information on the percentage of identified or reported cases of abuse in the general population (that is, with *base-rate information*). Or they may be presented with a single example of a welfare recipient who is abusing the system. In making decisions about using one over the other, reporters may fall victim to the tendency to regard base-rate information as less informative than concrete anecdotal information, even though the former is more valid and reliable.

This under-utilization of base-rate information is demonstrated in a study by Hamill, Wilson, and Nisbett (1980) from which the above example was drawn. Subjects read a vivid magazine article about a woman who had been living on welfare for many years but was clearly not a needy individual. The anecdotal case was presented along with base-rate statistics indicating that welfare recipients often take advantage of the system, that is, by statistics suggesting that welfare abuse is infrequent, implying that the reported case study was atypical. Despite the available base-rate information, subjects responded as if the case history were representative of welfare recipients in general. Even when contradicted by presumably valid statistical evidence, the catchiness of the case history had a greater impact on judgments.

In other research, investigators have found that concrete anecdotal information is more likely to be *remembered* than is base-rate data, again, even when it contradicts the wealth of statistical evidence (Taylor & Thompson, 1982).

The over-utilization of less reliable case information may be a function of the vividness or engaging quality of cases compared to base-rate information (Nisbett & Borgida, 1975; Nisbett & Ross, 1980), or a function of people's failure to see the relevance of base-rate data to their judgments about events (Tversky & Kahneman, 1978). In either case, journalists, like the subjects of psychologists' experiments, may over-utilize anecdotal data. Thus, when a source, intentionally or unintentionally, presents case information, journalists may regard it as sufficient evidence and not pursue more reliable base-rate information.

As an example of this phenomenon, the reporter for a small city newspaper took at face value the testimonial of a husband and wife that their mentally retarded son had improved dramatically since they instituted a very time-consuming physical therapy. The therapy involved exercising the child for most of the day to stimulate brain development.

Relying on these parents' very convincing report, and similar anecdotal information from a national organization devoted to promoting the therapy, the reporter wrote a glowing account of the therapy's benefits.[19] In the interest of "fairness," the reporter included a paragraph noting that many medical doctors were skeptical of the therapy's effectiveness, but he did not seek out base-rate information that would have been provided for him in the medical literature. Such information, in fact, cast doubt on the efficacy of the technique relative to more conventional therapies. Moreover, had the reporter pursued the matter, he would have learned that there are a number of alternative explanations to the parents' view that their child had improved significantly as a result of the therapy. That is, he may have improved, but he might have improved anyway, without this particular therapy; people with a strong belief that something will work may see more "progress" than really exists, etc.

Even when journalists behave differently and do provide base-rate information, they may not realize that the audience will give more weight to the anecdotal information and, if the anecdotal information and the base-rate information do not tell the same story, may draw erroneous conclusions.

Preference for Eyewitness Information

Psychologists who study the effects of eyewitness testimony in jury trials (Loftus, 1979) have found that jurors give more weight to the testimony of eyewitnesses than they do to other kinds of evidence. And this may be so, even though the perceptions of eyewitnesses may be biased in many of the ways we describe, and may in some cases be less (rather than more) reliable than other kinds of evidence. Recent research (Bell & Loftus, 1989) suggests that people may be especially likely to give weight to eyewitness accounts when such accounts contain a lot of detail. This may be true even when the details offered are seemingly insignificant and irrelevant to the observed event—such as the number of store items a customer dropped prior to a shoplifting incident.

If we can generalize from juries, we might expect journalists, too, to overvalue eyewitness accounts, particularly detail-laden accounts, leading to a greater likelihood of the selection of such accounts. Put another way, we might expect journalists, like juries, to assume that such eyewitness accounts offer more "truth" than they do, and so "count on" such accounts and perhaps prematurely limit their information gathering efforts.

Although we know of no evidence to support such speculations, it does seem to be the case that journalists intuitively understand the relative power of eyewitness accounts. Editors of newspapers and magazines so value first-hand reports that they often send their own reporters even when wire service reporters are on hand. Television journalists also appear to value eyewitness accounts, as evidenced by the number of six-o'clock news programs called "Eyewitness News."

Biases in Perceptions of Risk. In the wake of a growing interest in risk in recent years (the risk of diseases, nuclear war, acid rain, passive smoking), psychologists have done considerable research on people's perceptions of risk.

Among many other things, they have found that people overestimate the risk of death from dramatic or sensational causes, such as cancer, natural disasters, homicide, or accidents; conversely, people underestimate the risk of death from such undramatic causes as diabetes, emphysema, and asthma, causes that kill one person at a time and are common in nonfatal form (Slovic, 1986).

Thus, we might expect journalists preferentially to select information about deaths from dramatic or sensational causes over information about deaths from more pedestrian causes, even when the deaths from pedestrian causes prove the greater risk. That, in fact, is what some researchers have found (*e.g.*, Combs & Slovic, 1979), suggesting that journalists also process risk information in a biased manner. Indeed, it has been suggested that the biases prevalent in mass media accounts of risk are at least in part responsible for the biased perceptions of risk documented in the general public (Combs & Slovic, 1979).

In discussing biases and errors in the selection of information, it is important to note that journalists may fall victim to many other cognitive biases and errors not presented here. For a relatively complete review of such biases and errors, we refer readers to Fiske and Taylor (1984).

Chapter VII

Integration of Information

At some point, and probably at many points, in the process of producing news, the reporter must take all of the many and varied pieces of information collected and shape them into a reportable story. Thus, from discrete bits of evidence, and often from numerous perspectives, time frames, and venues, the reporter must create a consistent and coherent whole. In creating the final product, the reporter often has to integrate information to arrive at understandings about causal relationships. He often has to recollect information, contained either in notes or memory—a process that we now know is fraught with bias. Finally, the reporter must conclude the search for information. Psychologists have explored a number of factors that influence when ordinary people conclude their searches, and the influence of such factors on bias and error. Some of what they have learned may have a bearing on how journalists work as well.

Causal Linking of Events

Current research from numerous domains in social-cognitive and cognitive psychology—for example, research on how ordinary people explain events (Lalljee & Abelson, 1983; Leddo, Abelson, & Gross, 1984; Graesser & Black, 1985; Read, 1986; Einhorn & Hogarth, 1982), research that focuses on creating computer models of human cognitive processes (*e.g.*, artificial intelligence; see Shank & Abelson, 1977), and research dealing broadly with how people read and understand narratives (Bower, Black, & Turner, 1979; Black, Galambos, & Read, 1984)—provides converging evidence that the construction of causal sequences is basic to people's comprehension of events.

Illusory Correlation. Constructing links between events is so basic to understanding that people often impose relationships where none has been found to exist. The result of this tendency has been termed an *illusory correlation* (Chapman & Chapman, 1969). An excellent example of illusory correlation is found in the empirical work of Hamilton and Gifford (1976). Hamilton and Gifford reasoned that the rareness or infrequency of certain behaviors and the rareness or infrequency of certain racial, social, or ethnic groups may result in a pairing of these distinctive events.

To be less abstract, middle-class white people in this country rather infrequently encounter instances of negative social behaviors—aggressiveness, rioting, criminal actions. Moreover, most majority individuals infrequently encounter members of various racial or ethnic groups. In the minds of members of the majority, these two infrequent and distinctive events become paired such that they come to see a relationship (that is, an illusory correlation) between racial minorities and aggressive, undesirable behavior.

Further, majority group members may use this illusory correlation as the basis for other inferences about the social group. They may infer that minority members are likely to engage in negative behaviors and that the group can be characterized by predominantly negative traits. Thus, from an illusory correlation they may go on to make erroneous inferences and equally erroneous causal ascriptions.

One result of this bias may be for majority-dominated news media to highlight the negative behaviors of minority individuals, perpetuating these biased perceptions; thus, journalists may highlight the difficulties that individual minority athletes have with drugs and the police. A second result of this bias, of course, is to ascribe defining characteristics to groups for whom those descriptions are unwarranted. African-Americans as a group, for example, may be regularly and disproportionately associated with conflict, problems, illegality, and violence.

The Tendency to Oversimplify the Explanation of Complex Events. Another bias to which people fall victim when determining the causes of events is a tendency to oversimplify the explanation of complex events. This tendency is related to theory-confirming biases such that once people have developed a theory to explain the cause of an event, they will discount other contributing causes (Shaklee & Fischoff, 1977). So a journalist who attributes the cause of homelessness to failed mental health programs may discount other contributing causes. He thus may fail to see, and communicate, that homelessness is multiply determined.

The Fundamental Attribution Error. Some news events deal specifically with the actions of specific persons, either single individuals or groups. Stories revolve around the actions of heads of state, athletes, celebrities, the citizens of America, or the National Association for the Advancement of Colored People.

In seeking the causes of actions taken by individuals or groups, a person may include a set of factors not typically available when determining the causes of non-personal events. The causes of personal actions may be sought in the internal dispositions, abilities, or intentions of the actor. While it is not reasonable to seek the causes of a plummeting stock market in the intentions or inherent personality of the market (except perhaps in a metaphorical sense), personal actions are frequently and reasonably regarded as attributable to these internal characteristics.

The social-cognitive literature suggests that ordinary perceivers are imminently aware of personal dispositions when accounting for the causes of behavior on the part of persons or groups. Indeed, one of the most robust and pervasive cognitive biases is the tendency to overestimate the importance of personal or dispositional factors relative to external or situational factors in accounting for others' actions. This tendency to weigh personal causal variables more than situational variables is known as the fundamental attribution error. "Error" refers to the fact that this tendency to account for behavior by recourse to traits or dispositions frequently exists in situations in which environmental or situational forces have actually had an enormous impact on behavior.

The most frequently cited evidence for this bias is an empirical study by Jones and Harris (1967) in which perceivers drew personal inferences about a person who was responding to obvious situational constraints. In their study, Jones and Harris gave individuals (designated as "actors") explicit instructions to compose an essay supportive of Castro and Castro's Cuban policies. Actors, responding to these explicit instructions, and having no choice but to comply, completed the essay as instructed. The actors' essays, as required, included a number of pro-Castro remarks. The essays were subsequently given to another group of individuals whose task was to identify the true attitudes of the essay writers. All information regarding the essay writers' requirements to obey the instructions of the experimenter were given to this second group of readers.

Despite their knowledge of the situational constraints on the actors' behavior, readers of the essay inferred that the actors' true attitudes were pro-Castro. Had they taken account of the situational constraints on the essay writers (no-choice), they might have drawn different conclusions. Even when subjects themselves have determined the opinion that a person will express, they still have demonstrated a tendency to see the person as holding the opinion (Gilbert & Jones, 1986). Taken together, such studies demonstrate a tendency to draw personal inferences from an actor's behavior, while overlooking the environmental or situational factors that prompted, constrained, or produced that behavior.

Other studies have found evidence of the fundamental attribution error in role-playing contexts in which perceivers assume that behaviors falling in line with explicit role behavior or role constraints (*e.g.*, a librarian acting fastidious, or a police officer acting authoritative) represent the unique personality of the actor, when role constraints were an equally obvious and significant cause of that behavior (Ross, Amabile, & Steinmetz, 1977).

There are numerous examples of news items that appear to demonstrate this "dispositional" bias. Recall when Patricia Hearst, daughter of the publishing magnate Randolph Hearst, was kidnapped by the Symbionese Liberation Army, a revolutionary anarchist group. Ms. Hearst was held captive for many months in what many regarded as a precarious and life-threatening situation. She was forced by her captors to make favorable statements about the SLA anarchist cause, and after an extended ordeal of captivity, collaborated with her captors in a bank robbery. Reports about her actions frequently included statements that she was sympathetic to SLA ideology, and some even went so far as to find evidence of her sympathies in her pre-kidnapping behavior.

Like the constrained essay writer in the Jones-and-Harris study, it is more than reasonable to conclude that Ms. Hearst had no positive sentiments toward those who held her hostage and was acting in an extreme situation to protect her own life. Yet, these evident environmental constraints were minimized in favor of an accounting of her actions by recourse to stable, underlying dispositions. Indeed, readers revealed their own preference for dispositional accounting in regarding these character analyses as more compelling and informative than situation-based accounts.

Other examples of dispositional preference can be found in the often elaborate character analyses of prominent political figures, particularly those surrounding actions that violate social expectations. Former President Nixon's involvement in the Watergate break-in and subsequent cover-up may be reasonably and accurately attributed, at least in part, to extreme political pressures arising from his party, his advisers, and even his supporters in the general public. Yet, situational analyses were far less frequent than characterological analyses that stressed his presumed paranoia, political ambition, and insecurities.

In a related vein, Donohue, Olien, and Tichenor (1987) have pointed to the fact that the news media, in the aftermath of Contra-gate, appeared to focus more on the contributing role of individuals than on that of the underlying power structure. Thus, the media appeared to focus on the intellectual fitness and management style of former President Reagan, and on the behavior of other lower-level individuals, rather than on structural factors. They seem to have done this, despite the fact that, in addition to presidential leadership, an important factor investigated by the Tower Commission was the structure of the National Security Council.[20]

Similarly, in 1987, presidential candidate Gary Hart's extra-marital affairs were regularly attributed to his "motivations for self-sabotage," and not to the pressures of the campaign or the stresses of a rocky marriage.

The fundamental attribution error may show up in the assignment of credit as well as blame, as when a president gets the credit for an economic upswing that might have come about anyway, or when a mayor benefits from a reduction in crime over which he has had no control.

Unfortunately, this bias to find causes for actions in the dispositions of individuals may lead reporters to fail to acknowledge more complex, abstract, but nonetheless very real features of the context in which those actions take place, an oversight which may severely limit their audience's understanding of the multi-faceted, social surroundings in which news events are embedded.

Reconstruction and Hindsight Biases

At the time reporters write their stories, some of the information will be garnered from notes, tapes, and other records collected at the scene of the event itself. Some information will be derived from memories of the event—the mental pictures, images, and stored words that need to be recalled and reconstructed for the purpose of putting them into story form.

In recalling past events reporters may regard memorial information as accurate representations (even as exact copies) of the event itself. This may be true even when the stored information in memory consists of their own biased interpretations or evaluations of the event (Wyer, Srull, Gordon, & Hartwick, 1982; Wyer & Gordon, 1982).

Thus, if we observe an ambiguous bumping of a black student and a police officer at a student demonstration, and if we interpret that behavior as aggressive and infer or attribute hostile motivations to the student, at the time of recall those interpretations will be regarded as verbatim remembrances and not highly evaluative ones. Thus, the "facts" retrieved by the reporter may be highly constructed versions of the real event.

This bias, which is called *biased reconstruction,* can operate indepen-dently of encoding processes. Indeed it involves the reinterpretation of memorial information in light of new information or hypotheses about the event. In an early demonstration of this phenomenon, Snyder and Uranowitz (1978) asked people to read a narrative chronicling the life of a young woman. Participants in the study later learned that the woman was living either a lesbian lifestyle or a heterosexual lifestyle. This new knowledge exerted a powerful effect on channeling people's remem-brances of her life history as presented in the narrative.

For example, in reconstructing the life of the presumed lesbian, people identified her as having an abusive father, never having a steady boyfriend, never having dated, and being physically unattractive. The identical narrative produced the following reconstructions for the pre-sumed heterosexual woman: she had a tranquil childhood, dated fre-quently, had a steady boyfriend, and was rather attractive. The later-learned lifestyle information—the hypothesis and expectancies generated from that information—influenced previously learned factual information in a manner confirming and perpetuating, in this case, stereotypic beliefs.

Although subsequent studies have failed to replicate these particular findings with respect to the lesbian issue (Belleza & Bower, 1981; Clark & Woll, 1981),[21] other researchers (Loftus & Palmer, 1973; Croxton, Eddy, & Morrow, 1984) have found similar results in a variety of additional domains.

In one such demonstration, Ross, *et al.*(1981) generated attitudes about such common health-related activities as brushing one's teeth and showering. Later, in another context, they asked subjects to recall how often they had engaged in such activities during the previous two weeks. As expected, subjects who had been induced to have a negative attitude toward such activities in some cases "remembered" having engaged in them less often than those induced to have a positive attitude. So, subjects who had heard an expert rail against the value of brushing one's teeth, saying it erodes the enamel and damages the gums and leads to infection and tooth loss, reported that they had brushed their teeth less often during the prior two weeks than did subjects who had heard an expert sing the praises of brushing one's teeth.

A particularly vivid illustration of reconstruction bias outside of the laboratory is recounted in Myers (1987, pp.124-125). In the mid-1970s, according to one survey, a whopping 70 percent of Americans recalled having seen a televised replay of the assassination of President John F. Kennedy shortly after the event. In actuality, they could not have done so, for the film was not televised until 1976. People, it appears, simply reconstructed this memory, though they were not aware of that fact.

Related to reconstruction bias is *hindsight bias,* the tendency for people when retrospectively evaluating events or outcomes to exaggerate greatly the foreseeability of the events, and indeed often to see them as having been inevitable (Fischhoff & Beyth, 1975; Slovic & Fischhoff, 1977). People tend to overestimate what they would have known, believing they had known all along what was going to happen; in a similar vein, people generally overestimate what others *should* have known.

Leary (1982) demonstrated a kind of hindsight bias after President Reagan's landslide victory over Jimmy Carter in 1980. The day before President Reagan's election, when Leary asked people what they thought the outcome of the election would be, the average person foresaw a narrow victory for Reagan. However, the day after the election, when Leary asked other people what result they *would have predicted* prior to the election, most indicated that they had expected a larger victory for the president.

Hindsight bias can be expected to show up in journalism in a number of ways. It may be found in journalists' retrospective judgments that the outcome of an event was "predictable," though in fact it may not have been. As Myers (1987) has pointed out in connection with the Reagan landslide, commentators at the time—"forgetting that the election had been 'too close to call' until the final few days of the campaign"—in retrospect "found the Reagan landslide unsurprising and easily understandable" (Myers, 1987, p. 21).

Hindsight bias may also show up in journalists' *post hoc* analyses of the wisdom of actions and decisions. The ill-fated Iran rescue plan that is widely believed to have contributed to President Carter's loss in the

1980 election, was deemed after-the-fact to have been doomed from the start, though in actuality the plan may have appeared quite reasonable when it was initially implemented. In a related vein, George Bush's choice of Dan Quayle as a running mate may have seemed like a reasonable choice when the decision was first made. However, when assessed after the fact, with knowledge of the negative political and public response that followed, and of Quayle's rocky performance in the televised debate against Lloyd Bentsen and in dealing with the press, it appeared to many observers to be not only a dumb decision but also an *obviously* dumb decision.

In assessing the wisdom of various actions and decisions that led to specific outcomes, then, it may be extremely difficult for journalists to ignore what they know to have happened. Given this, we would expect journalists to make overly critical judgments of decisions and actions that ended badly (since the outcomes are seen as foreseeable or inevitable) and to make overly generous judgments of decisions and actions that ended well.

Concluding the Search

Reporters make decisions, implicit or explicit, about the investigation of an event—the sources to interview, the questions to ask, the leads to pursue. Of equal concern are decisions about when to conclude the investigation. Reporters must decide when to be open to information and also when all the information one needs for an accounting of an event is at hand. In a series of papers by Kruglanski (Kruglanski & Freund, 1982; Kruglanski, in press), it is suggested that decisions to be open or closed to information may depend on two, sometimes competing, needs—the need to make a decision or evaluation within an allotted time frame, and the need to avoid errors or mistakes. Kruglanski argues that when individuals face time pressures, they close off or "freeze" information gathering and evaluative processes more quickly than when time pressures do not exist. Contexts that arouse motivations to avoid error, or invalidity, he argues, have the opposite effect, decreasing the tendency to "freeze" information gathering. That is, if we desire to be accurate, we keep ourselves open to information longer and spend more time reflecting or evaluating information. Reporters seem to be caught in the difficult position of being both under salient time constraints and under enormous pressure to be accurate. Kruglanski's empirical work provides us with insights as to the nature of information gathering and conclusion drawing when these two competing forces operate simultaneously.

First, as Kruglanski predicts, when individuals desire to be accurate, they do indeed consider more pieces of information before drawing their conclusions. The desire to be accurate results in an extended "open" phase and more considered conclusions. But, if we add time pressure, it profoundly reduces people's openness to information. Under these conditions, people freeze off information gathering earlier and use a considerably more constrained and limited pool of information.

Moreover, when time constraints are imposed, despite competing needs for accuracy, information processing biases are profoundly increased. People are more likely to confirm initial hypotheses, more likely to attend only to hypothesis-consistent information, even when inconsistent information is clearly present, and they are less likely to consider alternative yet equally plausible hypotheses when evaluating and interpreting information. Thus, time pressures undermine motivations for accuracy, and have the effect of limiting information gathering, while also increasing many biases involved in the gathering and evaluation stages.

Kruglanski's data are particularly pertinent to the reporting process in that few reporters have the luxury of extended or generous amounts of time in which to get the information and report the story. Indeed, in telephone interviews with 48 Midwest journalists, Parsigian found that the most frequent reason given for ending information collection was the pressure of a deadline.[22] Under deadline pressures, the best intentions of the reporter to be fair and to be accurate may be undone by premature decisions to draw conclusions and release a story.

Chapter VIII

Interactions and Perseverance of Biases and Errors

One point to be highlighted before considering the implications of these findings is the multiplicity, and often interdependence, of the many cognitive biases and errors described here.

It should be clear from the discussion so far that cognitive processes do not flow in a simple or linear fashion. And, we may expect that for any news event to be reported, there may be a number of passes through the information processing cycle as new information is added, new events unfold, and new sub-tasks are undertaken by the reporter.

As we have seen, categorization clearly influences the theories that are generated, and existing theories influence questioning and information selection, and subsequently have an effect on the kinds of information retrieved and recalled. How reporters integrate information will be similarly affected by what is encoded at the time of the event and then retrieved and reconstructed at the moment the story is written.

It is also the case that information learned later can result in the generation of new categorizations and theories, dramatically influencing, even biasing, the nature of information already obtained and stored. It should be pointed out, though, that these later revisions in categorizations and theories have been found to occur most often when no initial hypotheses existed at the time the earlier information was encoded, or when the later information is so dramatic or extreme that the earlier information simply cannot be made to fit the initial categorizations. In most of the cases studied so far, there is a profound tendency toward the perseverance of those initial formulations. Thus, most of the biases operate in the service of preserving and elaborating initial perspectives, giving those initial views enormous importance when reporting the "facts" of the event (Ross, 1977; Ross, Lepper & Hubbard, 1975).

Chapter IX

Implications for the Study of Newswork

To what extent do the particular cognitive biases and errors that we have discussed actually show up in newsrooms?

While the examples we have used and the speculations we have made may be intuitively appealing, the answer is anything but clear. On the one hand, journalists are human beings, and to the extent that cognitive biases and errors are built into the cognitive system of human beings, we should expect journalists to reveal such biases. On the other hand, the laboratories of psychologists, while stripped of many of the complexities of everyday life, are not unconnected to environmental constraints; indeed, some cognitive biases and errors have been found to vary as a function of changes in the environment, which failures-to-replicate reveal only too well. Thus, we might expect cognitive biases and errors to show up across occupational settings (as indeed they do: see Sims, Gioia, & Associates, 1986; Rogoff & Lave, 1984). But we might also expect at least some of these biases and errors to vary as a function of the particular occupational and organizational constraints under which people work.

In journalism we have a situation where some occupational and organizational constraints might be expected to exacerbate normal cognitive biases, while others might be expected to minimize such biases. For example, journalists work under unusual production constraints, often including severe time pressures, which, as we have seen, can aggravate some of the biases described here. On the other hand, many journalists subscribe to professional norms associated with balance and fairness (Boyer, 1981); under some circumstances such norms could conceivably alleviate some of the cognitive biases we have described.

Clearly the need is for research on cognitive biases and errors in journalism. For starters, there is a need for research that simply describes how journalists actually process, and bias, the information that becomes news. In addition, there is a need for studies that more directly link the cognitive processing of journalists to environmental constraints; there is a need, in short, for investigations that explore the specific effects on journalists' information processing of such things as organizational constraints, news sources, community structure, culture, and professional norms. Finally, to the extent that journalists are discovered to exhibit the cognitive biases outlined here, and to the extent that such biases lead to judgments of "error," there is a need to determine if such biases are amenable to change.

Research on How Journalists Process Information

Many specific research questions can be generated by the foregoing speculations and review of selected research. Questions concerning how journalists process information include (but clearly are not limited to) the following:

Journalists' Categorizations. How do journalists categorize and subsequently label people, events, and phenomena? When information is missing, as it often is, particularly on breaking stories, do journalists make inferences or "fill in the blanks" in keeping with their categorization schemes, as we have speculated that Lindsy Van Gelder did in covering feminist demonstrations in the late 1960s? To what extent do category-based constructions lead reporters to make judgments about story subjects, implicitly in news stories or explicitly in editorials?

Journalists' Theories. In a related vein, how do journalists theorize about people and events that they have categorized? We have assumed, along with others, that in developing stories journalists do posit hypotheses about people and events. This is not an unreasonable assumption. However, it should be pointed out that some might not agree. For example, Curtis MacDougall, in his classic text, *Interpretative Reporting*, has argued: "The truth-seeking reporter...if he is operating correctly, has no predetermined ends to seek, no hypotheses to prove—just the truth to be determined" (MacDougall, 1982, p.12). Even if one takes such views to be naive—or purely ideological—it is not inappropriate to ask whether journalists do hypothesize about people and events prior to reporting. Cognitive psychologists have pointed to the need to learn about the pervasiveness of hypothesis testing, particularly among different occupational groups (Snyder & Gangestad, 1981). Research addressing this question should help meet that need.

In an exploratory effort to investigate this and related matters, Stocking and LaMarca (1989) persuaded reporters at a medium-sized city newspaper to describe briefly some of their non-breaking news and feature stories prior to reporting.

Their findings lend support to our assumption that journalists hypothesize about the people, organizations, events, and phenomena they intend to cover. Specifically, 81 percent of the story descriptions provided by reporters contained hypotheses, defined as tentatively held beliefs about story subjects,[23] and all of the journalists posited hypotheses in at least one of their descriptions.[24]

Interestingly, the journalists' story descriptions contained not only hypotheses but also assumptions, defined as unquestioned beliefs about story subjects.[25] To be more precise, virtually every story description contained assumptions about the people, organizations, events, and phenomena that reporters intended to cover. For example, in describing a story about a college coach, one reporter expressed his belief that the coach is "hated outside (the state), (and) seen as a rude, ugly American figure." And in a story about the use of computers in education, a reporter asserted that "Nobody questions computers in the classroom."

Most of the time, the assumptions appeared warranted; that is, they seemed "solid," or based on knowledge about which there seemed to be universal agreement (*e.g.*, the new president of the university is Jewish). However, sometimes the assumptions appeared to be based on more limited information or on judgments about which there might reasonably be expected to be disagreement. For example, the assumption that the college coach is hated and seen as a rude, ugly American figure, while believed by the reporter to be "solid," might be considered open to question, or "porous," by outsiders who do not share the world view of the reporter and his primary sources.

Given that journalists (at least under some circumstances) do theorize, what aspects of people and events do they theorize about? Stocking and LaMarca (1989) did not analyze their data with respect to this point. However, in his analyses of routine news content, van Dijk (1983) found that journalists regularly include information about the causes and consequences of events, leading us to infer that journalists hypothesize about causes and consequences of events prior to their reporting. In a related vein, Wiener (1985) reports several studies in which content analysis was done on sports and political news coverage for evidence of causal thinking. Such studies reveal pervasive attempts at explanations on the part of journalists, particularly when reporting outcomes that were unexpected (Lau & Russell, 1980), and when reporting failure as opposed to success (Lau, 1984; Foersterling & Groenvald, 1983).

In addition to hypothesizing about causes and consequences of behavior and events, journalists appear to hypothesize about people's characters. In a study that included an analysis of the *Chicago Tribune* during an election year, political scientist Doris Graber (1988) found a great deal of attention given to the personal qualities of political candidates for president. Specifically, Graber found that news accounts of presidential candidates paid more attention to candidates' personal qualities, such as trustworthiness, strength of character, and compassion, than to professionally relevant characteristics, such as the ability to keep the peace and manage domestic and foreign affairs. Thus, at least in presidential election campaigns, we can infer that reporters spend more time hypothesizing about a candidate's human qualities than about their professional competence.

In other research, Ettema and Glasser (1985), who interviewed a number of investigative reporters, have documented how such reporters develop and pursue explicit hypotheses concerning the culpability of the people and agencies they are investigating.

It is clear from these studies and from anecdotal evidence found in such things as the in-house manual of the *Wall Street Journal* noted earlier (Blundell, 1986) that journalists may theorize about many things as they set out to do their stories. But just what are these things? This appears to be a question that many researchers could answer, but have not thought much about.

Researchers appear to have given more thought to the content of journalists' assumptions. Some investigators (*e.g.*, Gans, 1980) have inferred from media content that American journalists share values, such as individualism, responsible capitalism, altruistic democracy, and ethnocentrism. From the cognitive perspective presented here, such values might be seen as general evaluative assumptions about the culture that journalists as a group tend to share. Other investigators, particularly those from the "critical" school of media analysis (*e.g.*, Hallin, 1989) have asserted that journalists, along with their sources, share assumptions about the boundaries of social and political normalcy.

To date, much of the discussion about shared journalistic assumptions has focused on those in conventional political and economic realms. Much less is known about shared assumptions in other arenas of life (sports, art, and science, for example). Nelkin (1987) has inferred from media coverage of science and technology that American journalists share assumptions about this realm. Journalists, she argues, tend to look at scientists as neutral sources of authority. They idealize science, seeing scientists as superior and isolated from the rest of us, and viewing science as a pure, dispassionate profession.

If what Nelkin says is correct, we would say that American journalists share underlying stereotyped-based assumptions about scientists, science, and technology. Nelkin's work is provocative. However, like Gans' work in the more conventionally political realm, and like the work of many critical scholars, it is also largely impressionistic, and is based on a limited sample of media content. There remains a great deal we still have to learn about journalists' shared assumptions about science and technology, and a whole range of other subjects as well.

There also is a great deal we do not know about the idiosyncratic assumptions of journalists in these various realms. Although surveys assessing journalists' general beliefs on topics tend to reveal considerable agreement (Olien *et al.*, 1989), they also reveal variance, at least some of which may be idiosyncratic to the individual. In studying cognitive processing in journalism, determining what is idiosyncratic may be just as interesting as determining what is not.

Moreover, just how such general assumptions, both shared and unshared, shape journalists' thinking about individual stories prior to reporting—how these very general beliefs play themselves out in specific hypotheses and assumptions about story subjects—is less clear. Studies that relate journalists' general assumptions to the more specific hypotheses and assumptions contained in journalists' story ideas might help sort some of this out.

Effects of Hypotheses and Assumptions on Newsgathering. How, if at all, do hypotheses/assumptions guide the newsgathering process? In the case of *hypotheses*, do they in fact guide, as we have speculated, the selection of sources? the types of questions asked? the evaluation of data? Do journalists seek and process information in a way that tends to confirm their hypotheses? in such a way, in other words, that there is a strong, positive relationship between evidence sought at each step of the newsgathering process, and evidence found?

And what is the effect of *assumptions* on newsgathering? As Stocking and LaMarca (1989) have pointed out, assumptions are by definition not questioned. If something is not questioned by a journalist, it is not likely to be tested. And if something is not tested, it may be very influential with respect to subsequent reporting. Although psychologists have not examined the effects of assumptions relative to hypotheses,[26] it is not unreasonable to expect that assumptions will be even more influential than hypotheses on information gathering.

In some cases, assumptions may affect both story definition and subsequent reporting. Thus, the reporter who assumes a coach to be hated around the country may strive to do a story on *how* the coach gives the school a negative national image, and to seek out sources (and ask questions) that will answer that basic question. By contrast, the reporter who questions *whether* a coach is hated around the country may be more likely to do a story on whether or not the coach gives the school a negative national image, and to seek out a range of sources (and ask a range of questions) that would provide him answers to that more open-ended question.

This is not to say that assumptions cannot be challenged, and stories redefined, in reporting. Indeed, although the reporter in our study did initially seek to find out the effects of the coach's assumed negative image, he ended up writing a story in which some of the evidence clearly refuted his assumption.[27]

Parsigian has some retrospective data that may bear on the effects of initial hypotheses and assumptions. She asked 48 journalists on papers in four metropolitan areas to describe the steps they went through in developing a self-assigned story. Although the study was not designed to test for confirmational strategies, her findings can be viewed as addressing our speculation that journalists seek and select information so as to confirm their initial thinking.

Specifically, subjects were asked if the outcome of their newsgathering (the information they had gathered) had met their expectations (that is, had confirmed their initial focus or approach).[28] Forty-one said yes. Seven said no. One of the seven said that the data collected gave even greater importance to the outcome than expected, and the other six said that the data they had collected negated their expectations. Even though the seven indicated that the outcome of their newsgathering efforts had not met their expectations, five nevertheless wrote leads that in some way reflected them.

These data appear to suggest that journalists rarely negate their initial notions during the course of newsgathering. Yet in another set of questions, 21 of the 48 journalists reported that they had modified their initial direction (or "approach" in the words of the interview guide) on the strength of data gathered.

In personal correspondence, Parsigian has clarified this apparent contradiction. Of the 21 journalists who said they had modified their approach, some had made modifications at the outset of their investigations; since these modifications came early (or at least not late) in the reporting process, these reporters apparently identified them as part of their "initial" direction, and so, in response to the question that asked whether their newsgathering had confirmed their initial direction, answered in the affirmative. The reporters who modified their approaches toward the end of their investigations, by contrast, could more readily see that what they ended up with was not what they had started out with, and so reported, in response to the earlier question, that the outcome of their newsgathering had *not* met their initial expectations.[29]

Taking the responses to these questions together, it would appear that while most (41) journalists in this study reported outcomes that confirmed their initial direction, a sizable minority (21) also reported having made modifications in the act of reporting. Of these, most said that they did so early on or toward the middle of their investigations, while a few claimed that they modified near the end.

Parsigian's is not the only work that sheds light on these questions. The work of Ettema and Glasser (1985), although not framed in a contemporary cognitive perspective, is also relevant. Using intensive interviews, they describe the reporting method of one investigative reporter. Early on in an investigation, they found that the reporter typically spends time collecting evidence that will show that a tip is "real" and that a plan can be developed "for collecting enough additional evidence to make a case for the truth of an implied story" (p. 193). In "pitching" the story, or seeking justification for continuing, the reporter, in effect, actively seeks out evidence that tends to confirm the initial story tip.

Once given the go-ahead, the reporter, according to Ettema and Glasser, does not ignore disconfirming evidence. Indeed, the authors say that the reporter "must honestly seek out such evidence," which he then weighs. If, "in this weighing exercise, the scale tips decisively toward the exculpatory evidence or if, after much effort, the scale cannot be made to tip, the investigation is abandoned. If, however, the scale tips decisively toward the inculpatory evidence, the investigation finally becomes a story" (p. 196).

Finally, once the story is assembled, the reporter subjects the story to a "moral certainty test" in which he actively attempts to "generate alternative explanations or additional exculpatory evidence which could disconfirm the story" (p. 199).

To summarize Ettema and Glasser in the context of confirmational tendencies, the investigative reporter whom they interviewed reported a tendency toward active confirmation early in an in-depth investigation, a tendency to gather and weigh both confirming and disconfirming evidence during reporting, and a tendency toward active disconfirmation once the investigative story has been assembled.

Obviously, it is difficult to make much of the findings from these two studies. Neither investigation was designed to address specific questions of "confirmation bias." The object and nature of the reporter's beliefs are not always clear. Moreover, the data obtained in both studies are retrospective, subject to all the biases of such data; they are also based on small, non-random samples. It does appear, though, that confirmational tendencies are evident in at least some journalists' stories and some stages of reporting. Researchers would do well to try to pin down the circumstances in which confirmation bias does and does not occur in journalism.

Using interview and archival data on journalists' beliefs gathered prior to reporting, and additional data on journalists' subsequent information gathering, Stocking has begun to pin down evidence on confirmational bias (1989b). Preliminary findings from this work appear to be consistent with those from earlier studies. That is, confirmational tendencies appear to show up in some stories, but not in others. Perhaps even more interestingly, in stories in which they do show up, they show up at some, but not all, decision points.

Consider just the source selection decisions in a feature story on men and abortion. The story in question was written during the summer of 1988 when several men around the country were bringing lawsuits to prevent their mates from having abortions. By his own account, the reporter on this story had "very strong" feelings of opposition toward abortion. Thus, he was aware of a strong underlying evaluative belief that might lead him to the biased pursuit and selection of information.

However, he also professed to have a strong desire to avoid having his belief color his reporting. In fact, in an effort to prevent his anti-abortion stance from affecting his work, this reporter consciously avoided using tell-tale language in a classified ad he placed to solicit men willing to talk about their mates' abortions; more precisely, he took care not to use words that would conjure up "fathering" and "children" on the part of those who read the ad. In gathering general commentary on the issue of men and abortion, he also took care to solicit the views of both pro-life and pro-choice sources in the community. Thus, at some decision points, the reporter was able, in his own words, "to exempt" his beliefs, or not let them bias his sourcing decisions.

On the other hand, at other decision points, the reporter did not seem able to prevent his underlying evaluative belief about abortion from affecting his decisions. In describing his original story idea, the journalist hypothesized with what appeared to be a great deal of certainty that men must have feelings when their mates have abortions; at the same time, however, he articulated a specific competing hypothesis—that they may not. In spite of this competing hypothesis, the ad the reporter placed clearly restricted the range of men likely to respond—to men with feelings: "XX (reporter's name) of the XX (newspaper) is interested in speaking to men whose girlfriends or wives have had an abortion and who would be willing to talk anonymously about their feelings about the incident for a…story."

Although, theoretically, men with positive feelings could answer this ad just as well as men with negative feelings, it seems probable that men who felt badly about the experience would be more likely to respond than those with positive feelings, out of a presumably greater need to talk about their feelings. In fact, of the four who answered the ad, all expressed that they had been bothered by the abortions of their mates, though two indicated they were now at peace with the decision. Of the two who remained bothered by the abortion, one reported he had a recurring nightmare in which he is holding his newborn child, trying to protect him from some great danger. For the twelve years since his girlfriend had an abortion,[30] this man has awakened on a regular basis, shaking with fright because, in his words, "the danger—the thing out there—has taken the life of my child." This man and his nightmare became the lead for the story and the subject of an accompanying illustration.

It was only later, when the story was finished, that the reporter realized the biasing effect of the ad. At the time he ran the ad, it had not occurred to him that it would restrict the range of men who might answer. Apparently unwittingly, his ad sought sources that would confirm what we might reasonably assume (given his strong underlying views on abortion) to be the more strongly held hypothesis—namely, that men have feelings when their mates have abortions; it did not seek sources that might confirm his own articulated alternative hypothesis—that they may not.

Just why this reporter's underlying belief appeared to bias some source selection decisions and not others is an interesting question. As discussed at greater length elsewhere (Stocking, 1989b), it would appear that the reporter defined some of the sourcing decisions as requiring conscious efforts to avoid bias, whereas others he did not. Furthermore, whether or not he defined some of the sourcing decisions as requiring such vigilance appeared to be a function, at least in part, of prior sensitization on these matters.

Case studies such as this one are provocative, but they are obviously limited. Many more studies are needed to examine the effects not only of underlying evaluative beliefs but also of underlying descriptive beliefs about how the world works. Also, in line with previous suggestions, additional research is needed to understand how underlying beliefs of both types relate to the specific hypotheses and assumptions about story subjects that reporters take into their reporting,[31] and how these more specific hypotheses and assumptions guide subsequent information gathering. The foregoing case study explored the effects of an underlying evaluative belief and story-specific descriptive hypotheses on source selection decisions. That is a good beginning. However, we must also explore the effects of such beliefs, both shared and unshared, on a whole range of reporting and writing decisions, including the questioning of sources, the evaluation and selection of information obtained from these sources, and the use of such information.

Do Confirmational Strategies Lead to Error? To the extent that journalists do use theory-confirming strategies in newsgathering, do such strategies lead to outcomes that are in error? Stocking (1989a) has speculated that many of the initial "errors" in media coverage of the nuclear disaster at Chernobyl (including the blaming of the disaster on reactor construction rather than human error) may have resulted from journalists' use of confirmational strategies.

But, clearly, whether or to what extent theory-confirming strategies lead to "errors" in journalists' accounts is an empirical question. One of the difficulties in trying to answer such questions lies in determining what is meant by "error." In the analysis of Chernobyl coverage, a conclusion was judged in error if subsequent disclosures seemed to prove it wrong (as was the case with reports of casualties and causes of the disaster); a conclusion also was judged in error if, as in one case (the conclusion that information was not forthcoming from the Soviet Union because that country is a closed society), it was deemed wrong by parties not cited in the news media.

However, as "error" studies reviewed by Meyer (1987, pp.191-195) reveal, journalistic inaccuracies may be defined in several ways, depending on who is making the accuracy judgments. They may be defined as outcomes that journalists and sources might come to agree are inaccurate (a relatively small proportion of the errors identified by sources); as outcomes that sources believe are inaccurate (journalists may or may not agree; in fact, research on journalistic errors suggests that sources and journalists usually disagree about what constitutes an inaccuracy); or as outcomes that uninvolved judges, evaluating the evidence, would say are inaccurate. As a practical matter we would add that errors are often defined as outcomes that interested parties who are NOT quoted as sources believe are inaccurate.

In the story on men and abortion discussed earlier, sources, not surprisingly, differed in their evaluations of the story, with pro-choice sources seeing the story as less accurate and the reporting as worse (in terms of seeking out the right sources, asking or appearing to ask the right questions, interpreting or appearing to interpret the evidence properly) than did pro-life sources. Two social scientists who had done research on men and abortion, and one who had not (but who was familiar with such research), also saw the article as noticeably less accurate and less well-reported than did pro-life sources (Stocking, unpublished data). Interestingly, the reporter, in the absence of complaints (phone calls, letters, or letters-to-the editor) from either side of the abortion debate, inferred the story to be "objective."[32]

However error is defined (and there are merits and weaknesses to each definition), the question of whether or to what extent "errors" result as a consequence of hypothesis-confirming strategies awaits research.

Selection Biases. In selecting information from observations, interviews and documents, do journalists fall victim not only to confirmation bias but also to the other cognitive biases and errors reviewed in this paper? For example, do journalists also underutilize base-rate information relative to anecdotal information? Do they preferentially attend to contextually salient people, actions, and events in their reporting, and make extreme judgments about them, as we speculated was the case in journalists' coverage of Jesse Jackson during the 1984 and 1988 presidential races? Do journalists, like juries, tend to give more weight to eyewitness accounts than to other kinds of evidence? Do they overestimate the risk of death from dramatic or sensational causes? As noted earlier, there is some preliminary evidence (Combs & Slovic, 1979) that they do.

Biases in Information Integration. Finally, in integrating different pieces of the information mosaic, do journalists process information in such a way that they impose relationships where none may exist (illusory correlation)? Do they likewise oversimplify explanations of complex events? Do they fall victim to fallacies of causal reasoning, attributing sources' behavior to dispositional, rather than situational, causes, for example? Do they fall victim to reconstruction and hindsight biases as they sit down at their computer terminals to put together a story?

Research on Effects of Environmental Factors on Information Processing

In addition to research that simply describes how journalists process information, we need, as indicated earlier, to explore the specific effects of a range of environmental constraints on journalists' information processing. These include (but are not limited to) organizational constraints, news sources, community structure, culture, and professional norms.

Effects of Organizational Constraints. How and to what extent do organizational constraints shape the cognitive processes identified in this monograph?

In recent years, there has been an increasing recognition on the part of cognitive psychologists that people's goals play an important role in how information gets processed (Higgins, King, & Mavin, 1982). Although an individual's goals may differ to some degree from an organization's goals, often they do not. Indeed, it has long been known that journalists absorb the goals and policies of their organizations (Breed, 1955).

Thus, if the goal of an organization is to produce stories that will interest a particular set of consumers whom advertisers wish to reach, we would expect that journalists in the organization would process information in such a way that helps to meet that goal. Put in the framework we have presented here, we might expect reporters to generate hypotheses that make for "good stories" for that audience. Moreover, to the extent that journalists exhibit confirmation bias, we might expect them to seek information preferentially (via selection of sources, questions asked, etc.), and preferentially to select information that makes for "good stories."

Thus, if a major goal of a magazine is to appeal to an audience of leftists, we would expect journalists to perceive a need to generate hypotheses that members of the political left would find appealing, and to seek preferentially (select sources, ask questions, etc.) and select information that would confirm such hypotheses. By the same token, if a major goal of a magazine is to appeal to the broadest range of people in a community or culture, we would expect journalists to generate hypotheses supportive of the status quo, and (in the same ways) to seek and select information consistent with such notions. In other words, we would expect hypothesis-confirming biases in information seeking and selection, to the extent that they occur, to be in line with organizational goals. To the extent that they are not in line with such goals, we would expect them to be self-censored by the reporter; or if not self-censored, then we would expect them to be noticed, corrected, and even punished by others in the organization. Obviously, such expectations are hardly new or surprising; sociologists of the news have been making similar points for a long time. The difference, perhaps, is that we can now be more precise about the psychological mechanisms that allow organizational factors to have their effects.

In exploring organizational constraints on journalists, we might also ask how, and to what extent do time and space constraints (and other technological constraints) exacerbate the cognitive biases we have described?[33] Are journalists less likely to fall prey to cognitive biases when they have more time to work on stories? The work by Kruglanski and his colleagues reviewed earlier provides strong evidence that time pressures exacerbate processing biases. However, it might be that journalistic ways of doing things are so hardwired that reporters, no matter how much time they have, operate much the same way, purely out of habit.

There is some evidence that is consistent with the view that time constraints exacerbate cognitive biases in newsgathering. In studies of newspaper and wire service reporters, Fico and his colleagues have found that journalists' workload relates negatively both to number of sources selected (Fico, 1984a,b) and to story balance (Lacy, Fico, & Simon, in press). In other words, the more stories a journalist has to write (and presumably, then, the tighter the time constraints), the fewer the sources and the less likely the story is to be balanced.

Effects of News Sources, Community Structure, and Culture. In a related vein, how, and to what extent do news sources, community structure, and cultures shape journalists' information processing? Obviously, traditional work on newsmaking, journalists, and media content offer starting points.

Consider news sources, including those who routinely supply the press with "information subsidies" (Gandy, 1982). To date, most of the research examining the influence of sources and information subsidies on media content has been concerned with story selection (*e.g.*, VanSlyke Turk, 1986). But what about the influences on journalists' thinking after stories have been selected? Do sources structure thinking? Do they not only tell journalists what to think about but also *how* to think?

Van Dijk (1988a) has found that journalists often structure news episodes as their sources do, suggesting that sources may provide the structural framework for the telling of such episodes. Using the perspective we have presented here, we might ask some additional questions: Do sources "prime" reporters with respect to categories? to story-specific hypotheses and assumptions? perhaps even to the questions used to test hypotheses? Do they dictate the selection of data by taking advantage of the cognitive biases we have identified? by making generous use of anecdotal information relative to base-rate information, for example? or in the assignment of causes, by drawing more attention to individuals than to structures?

Research also would do well to consider the influence of community structure and culture on information processing. In a study of newspaper editors' perceptions of community planning, Olien *et al.*, (1989) found that editors' definitions of community planning varied in part as a function of the level of pluralism in their communities. So, editors in pluralistic communites[34] were more likely than editors in less pluralistic communities to define community planning as a strategy to promote order, control the impact or direction of change, and coordinate growth; conversely, journalists in less pluralistic communities were more likely to define community planning as a means of economic growth.

Given this difference in perception (which, using the perspective we have presented here, might be seen as a difference in underlying assumptions), we might expect journalists in more pluralistic communities to generate story-specific hypotheses that are supportive of "control" definitions; at the same time, we might expect journalists in less pluralistic communities to generate story-specific hypotheses that are supportive of "growth" definitions.

Moreover, to the extent that journalists exhibit confirmation bias in information gathering, we would expect them to do their reporting in ways that confirm these story-specific hypotheses. Thus, we would expect journalists from pluralistic communities preferentially to select "control" sources, preferentially to ask "control-related" questions, to give more weight to "control" evidence, etc. In a related vein, we would expect journalists from less pluralistic communities preferentially to select "growth" sources, preferentially to ask "growth-related" questions, to give more weight to "growth" evidence, etc.

In the same study, Olien and her colleagues found that editors' definitions of planning also varied as a function of ideological emphases in the larger social system. To be more exact, they found that as the general social system reduced federal funding and support for social planning during the Reagan years, editors' definitions of social planning also shifted, independent of the level of pluralism in the community. Olien *et al.* attributed this shift to a growing interdependence of local communities with the larger social system. Assuming communities continue to be interdependent in this way, we would expect journalists' hypothesis-generation and hypothesis-testing about community-level issues to also be in keeping, at least to some extent, with the ideology of the larger system.

Effects of Journalistic Norms and Practices. Finally, we might ask about the effects of journalistic norms and practices on cognitive bias and error. In psychology labs, students succumb to cognitive biases and errors even when instructed to be "objective." Does the same hold true for journalists, or do the norms relating to objectivity and fairness in journalism work against at least some of these biases?

The presence of such norms in mainstream American journalism is not hard to document. For example, survey research has shown that mainstream newspaper editors, if they do not as a body value "objectivity," do value fairness and balance (Boyer, 1981). Also, a good many documents of the occupation codify the general expectation that journalists will make efforts to be "objective." Typical is one industry-wide code of ethics that says objectivity is "a standard of performance toward which we strive" (The Society of Professional Journalists/Sigma Delta Chi, 1987).

Many of the codes go further to specify practices to which journalists should adhere as they strive to "serve the truth." Some of these seem especially relevant to the theory-confirming biases described earlier. For example, nearly all the codes of ethics for the field contain some warning against the injection of unlabeled opinions into news reports, and against unfair, one-sided accounts. The previously mentioned code of ethics, for example, says that "sound practice makes clear distinction between news reports and expressions of opinion. News reports should be free of opinion or bias and represent all sides of an issue."

In journalism, there is also the general expectation that journalists will not be overly driven by preconceived ideas. In the words of the in-house manual for reporters on the *Wall Street Journal*: "...a reporter must never hold inflexibly to his preconceptions, straining again and again to find proof of them where little exists, ignoring contrary evidence and passing up chances to explore fruitful areas that didn't figure in his early thinking:...events, not preconceptions, should shape all stories in the end" (Blundell, 1986, p.25).

Although research has found that journalists when making decisions rarely consult documents that codify the expectations of their occupations (Morgan, 1989), reporters nevertheless are sensitized to such expectations from the first day they set foot in a journalism classroom or newsroom. Even if they do not believe in the possibility of objectivity, journalists quickly learn the specific practices that at least superficially service these norms. Some of these practices—such as a pro-and-con kind of balancing of conflicting views—become so ingrained, according to sociologist Gaye Tuchman, that they are used almost "ritualistically" to ward off charges of bias (Tuchman, 1972).

Obviously, mainstream American journalists receive far more than a simple lab instruction to be "objective" when they set out to report the news. Most carry with them a long-standing set of expectations, a repertoire of specific practices, and repeated experience in employing these practices. In addition, journalists often work under the expectation that they will be subjected to a form of editorial review, either from editors, or from fact-checkers, individuals whose job it is to check each fact in a story.

To be sure, one cannot expect such expectations and practices to guarantee fairness and balance. As Hallin has pointed out, there may be some people and perspectives in the news about which there appears to be so much supportive consensus ("motherhood and apple pie") that journalists "do not feel compelled either to present opposing views or to remain disinterested observers. On the contrary, the journalist's role is to serve as an advocate or celebrant of consensus values" (Hallin, 1989, p. 117).

Likewise, there may be other people and perspectives in the news about which there appears to be so much negative consensus (terrorists or communism, for example) that journalists do not feel compelled to try to be objective. Concerning those who violate or challenge consensus, journalists under these circumstances play the role of "exposing, condemning, or excluding ... those who violate or challenge the ... consensus" (Hallin, 1989, p. 117).[35]

Put another way, there may be some beliefs about which there is so much perceived consensus (positive or negative) that journalists hold the beliefs without question, as assumptions.[36] With assumptions, unlike hypotheses, there is no possibility of entertaining alternative beliefs; indeed, under such circumstances, as Chomsky has suggested, alternatives may be beyond the "bounds of thinkable thought" (Chomsky, 1985). In the absence of an awareness of competing alternatives, journalists may perceive no need to invoke journalistic norms and practices to insure fairness and balance.

On the other hand, Hallin notes that there are other people and perspectives about which there obviously is less consensus (Republicans/Democrats, pro-abortion/anti-abortion).[37] With these people and perspectives, journalists do feel compelled to try to be objective. Put in the framework we have provided here, they feel compelled to entertain alternative viewpoints, or at the very least to "balance" them.

Thus, although one might not expect journalistic norms and practices to minimize biases in arenas where there is a large amount of perceived consensus, they conceivably could have some effects on matters of apparent "legitimate controversy." At the very least, given the apparent pervasiveness of journalism norms and practices associated with fairness and objectivity, it may be risky simply to assume that journalists will reveal hypothesis-confirming biases as do lay subjects in psychologists' labs.

By discussing the effects of the foregoing environmental constraints on cognitive processing separately, we do not mean to imply that such constraints operate independently of each other. To the contrary, in their interaction they may have varying effects on how journalists process information.

Consider the joint influences of news sources and news organizations. Conceivably, the influence of news sources will vary as a function of the organizational constraints under which journalists work. In situations where journalists are highly pressed for time, for example, we might expect source influence on cognitive processing to be greater than under circumstances where journalists are less pressed. Thus, in heavy workload environments, such as those that might be found at small newspapers or small television outlets, we might expect journalists to adopt source perspectives "whole cloth," entertaining them less as hypotheses than as assumptions; conversely, in light workload environments, such as those that might be found at large metropolitan newspapers or large urban television stations, we might expect journalists to do more questioning of source perspectives, entertaining them more as hypotheses, with the predicted effects on subsequent information gathering.[38]

Other Research Needs: Are Biases and Errors Amenable to Change?

Assuming that journalists, like lay perceivers, succumb to the cognitive biases and errors identified and described here, and assuming that such biases and errors lead to accounts that are deemed problematic, can something be done? Can such biases and errors be avoided or minimized?

To answer the question, we need first to draw a distinction between processes that researchers have regarded as automatic and those thought to be controlled. Automatic processes are spontaneous processes that seem to occur without explicit awareness or deliberate decision. They are adaptations to our limited processing capabilities that allow us to attend to more than one thing at once. Driving, once it has been learned and practiced at great length, becomes an automatic process. When we drive, we don't have to think about driving; we just drive and think about other things.

In the context we have presented here, we might classify as automatic the processes of categorization and hypothesis-generation when the real-world event is familiar, or when the categorization mode is used frequently by the perceiver. Also in this class we might find confirmational tendencies in the observation of complex ongoing sequences of events and saliency biases. In addition, we might find some biases in retrieval and recall, such as the tendency to regard memory-based information as that which actually appeared in the event.

Because automatic processes are ones that have been deeply learned, and because they operate outside of our awareness, they can be difficult to disrupt. Indeed, automatic processes are by some researchers' definitions inescapable and unlikely to be redressable, at least readily. So, we may have to accept their presence across the domains in which people deal with social stimuli, and that includes reporters relaying to us the events of an enormous and complex world.

We can take a more optimistic stance with regard to biases that are the result of more controlled processes—those processes that perceivers direct and engage in by deliberate decision. In this class we may include biases from categorization and hypothesis-generation when the real-world event is novel or unexpected, and some confirmational tendencies, including those related to decisions about the range or form of the questions posed. We may also include some biased decisions about the types of evidence to be used to illustrate a story, such as decisions to use single-case material over base-rate data. Also redressable perhaps are perceivers' tendencies to overemphasize dispositional information over situational information.

Certainly, some research has suggested that some of the biases we have described in this paper can be minimized. For example, simply telling people to be unbiased will not lessen people's tendency to maintain a theory in the face of disconfirming evidence. However, telling people to consider carefully how they are evaluating evidence, and to watch their biases as they go through the process of interpreting data, will minimize biases (Lord, Lepper, & Thompson, 1980). So also will asking people to explain why their theory might be wrong (C. A. Anderson, 1983). The use of nondirectional questions has also been found to solicit information that can effectively reduce theory-confirming biases (Trope & Bassok, 1982).

As we have noted, it is also reasonable to suppose that professional norms and practices can sometimes minimize confirmation bias. The need to provide a report that will pass the editorial scrutiny of editors and fact-checkers may also have similar effects. Indeed, there is evidence in some studies that when motiviation is sufficient, people can forgo or disrupt even those biases associated with the more entrenched automatic processes (Branscombe, 1989).

But this optimism must be tempered by important qualifications. First, research has shown that attempts to minimize or reverse cognitive biases through explicit training or other procedures frequently fail. (See, for example, Wilder & Allen, 1978; Hayden & Mischel, 1976; Ross, Lepper, & Hubbard, 1975; Jones, 1979.) Moreover, procedures that have been effective in reversing some of these biases are often heavy-handed, elaborate, and temporary.

For example, in a study by one of the present authors (Gross & Darley, in review), an attempt was made to reverse perceivers' theory-confirming biases, in this case hypotheses derived from social stereotypes. Attempts at explicit training with regard to the pitfalls and consequences of theory-confirmation biases failed. The procedure that proved effective was one in which perceivers were given a three-page information package designed to replace their original hypothesis with an alternative, non-stereotypical hypothesis.

The procedure did cause perceivers to invoke this new hypothesis, but did so by thrusting it upon the hapless perceivers, who probably would not have generated that hypothesis on their own. Moreover, the effects were transitory; perceivers used their alternative hypothesis within the immediate context, but did not generalize it to other situations.

Finally, we must temper any optimism about the minimization or reversal of biases in light of the environmental constraints under which journalists work. Many of these constraints, as we have noted, may serve to increase, not reduce, the cognitive biases we have identified. Also, it is clear that neither professional norms and practices nor expectations of editorial review are sufficient completely to eliminate such biases, as the first author has seen in her own case studies (Stocking, 1989b).

Moreover, psychologists have documented a tendency for people to overestimate the accuracy of their judgments (Fischhoff, Slovic, & Lichtenstein, 1977). To the extent that journalists fall victim to this "overconfidence phenomenon," we might expect them to be resistant to efforts to improve their thinking.

Obviously, only further research can determine the extent to which the cognitive biases and errors that we document in journalism are amenable to change.

A Word on Method

In documenting cognitive biases and errors in newsmaking, in linking such biases more directly to environmental factors, and in trying to determine the extent to which such biases are amenable to change, we would do well to employ a diversity of research methods. A diversity of methods may be especially useful in taking the first critical step of documenting cognitive biases and errors in journalism.

Although content studies are obviously limited in what they can tell us about how journalists think, an argument can be made that such analyses, particularly those developed from a contemporary cognitive perspective, are important beginnings. For example, fine-grained studies of media content can help us begin to determine the aspects of people and events that journalists theorize about, and to identify categories and theories as revealed in metaphors, story foci or "themes," and story construction. Content analyses can also help us to gain insights into how journalists treat evidence in text (how they handle anecdotal evidence and base-rate information, for example), how they assign cause or blame, etc. Some of this work has already begun.

As we have noted, some psychologists have already begun to document the pervasiveness of causal thinking in journalism (Lau, 1984; Lau & Russell, 1980; Foersterling & Groenvald, 1983).

In a wide-ranging program of research, van Dijk is examining the content and structure of news articles using both linguistic and cognitive units of analysis (van Dijk, 1983, and 1988a, b). In some of this work, van Dijk has analyzed news content about ethnic minority groups, drawing inferences about the "social representations" of these groups among journalists. Among other things, he has found that ethnic groups, or race relations in a multi-ethnic society, are regularly associated in the press with conflict, problems, and difficulties, if not with violence and illegality (van Dijk, 1988b).

The news media, when they do provide information that runs counter to such representations, "at the same time provide the argumentative strategies that can 'handle' them so they can be discounted" (van Dijk, 1988b, p. 207). Putting this work into the framework we have provided here, we may say that van Dijk has begun to infer some of the shared categories and theories that journalists use, and some of the ways that reporters discount evidence that does not confirm such theories. Furthermore, he has begun to show how such theories may play themselves out structurally and stylistically.

In addition to content analytic work, we need, of course, to get access to what journalists actually think as they engage in tasks to produce the news. We need to observe reporters as they observe events, talk with sources, and peruse documents, and, when possible, get the reporters to talk about what they are thinking as they go about the business of newsgathering.

Protocol analysis, in which the investigator talks with subjects while they are performing tasks (Ericsson & Simon, 1984), is one methodological tool that may be used to gain access to journalists' thoughts. To date, protocol analysis has been used extensively in investigations of the writing of basic compositions (Hayes & Flower, 1986) and in studies of the writing of journalistic stories (Pitts, 1982). However, it might also be used in studies of the reporting (as distinct from writing) of journalistic pieces. That is, investigators might talk with journalists as they go about the business of developing theories about people and events; finding and evaluating sources; and accepting, rejecting, or supplementing information supplied by sources.

In those situations in which it would be impossible to talk with reporters engaged in newsgathering (as in the middle of an interview with a source), investigators could ask journalists to tape their encounters. Alternatively, they could ask journalists to reconstruct their newsgathering, prompted by their own notes, immediately following the performance of a newsgathering task; these retrospective accounts could then be checked against comparable accounts by sources. The work of the first author, noted earlier, has taken this latter route (Stocking & LaMarca, 1989).

Obviously, there are limitations to trying to get journalists to talk about mental processes. As Nisbett and Wilson (1977) discuss in a controversial article, some of these processes operate below the level of consciousness, with the result that verbal reports on mental processes will not always provide an accurate account of the processes that were, in fact, operating. Still, there can be some value in this enterprise. For instance, in talking to journalists as they decide what to "focus" on, we may gain insights, albeit primitive, into how reporters categorize and theorize about people and events. Similarly, in talking to them as they evaluate, accept, reject, and supplement information, we may gain insights into the decision rules that they routinely employ as they process information.

At the very least, we will gain insights into what journalists *think* they are thinking, which, when coupled with systematic observations by investigators, could provide data of great use to those seeking to minimize or eliminate errors in journalists' thought processes. The real value of this kind of analysis lies not in its usefulness in testing theory rigorously, but, as Pitts (1982) has pointed out, in exploratory studies describing uncharted territory or creating taxonomies or hypotheses.

Not only would it be helpful to conduct new studies in which we observe reporters and talk with them as they go about the business of reporting, but it would also be of value to examine existing observational studies in light of emerging cognitive perspectives. A number of the more recent observational studies by sociologists (Fishman, 1980; Gans, 1980; Tuchman, 1978; and Gitlin, 1980), while they explain their findings in terms of environmental factors, in fact contain given a great deal of attention given to cognitive issues.

Fishman (1980), in particular, reveals an interest in how journalists think, and repeatedly uses examples that illustrate the basic cognitive biases that psychologists have documented in experimental studies. For instance, he notes that once, when a police report failed to say anything about clues in a case, a reporter, drawing on his knowledge of typical police reports, inferred that the absence of knowledge meant something (there are no clues), and used that subsequent inference in his story. To a cognitive psychologist, this might be an illustration of journalistic inference-making based on a cognitive theory.

There is another value to reexamining old observational studies from a cognitive perspective. In so doing, we may begin to see that a cognitive perspective both helps us to understand better how environmental influences come to have their effects and also, in some cases, provides a plausible (and testable) alternative explanation for journalists' behavior. Some of the behavior that Fishman (1980) reports as a product of the "news production process" (a reporter ignores police statistics that show a crime wave is NOT taking place) may also be understood as a product of how people, in general and independent of newsroom influences, think. This is not to say, as we have noted repeatedly, that environmental influences have no bearing on cognitive bias and error. Indeed, as we have indicated, environmental influences may significantly exacerbate or minimize some biases. It is merely to say that there may be much more going on here than studies from a purely environmental perspective would suggest.

Of course, we also need to move beyond descriptive fieldwork to experiments in which we can more rigorously test cause-effect relationships. For reasons of external validity, field experiments would be ideal, of course. Thus, we might assess journalists' beliefs prior to the reporting of a planned event (such as a university press conference announcing the latest development in an ongoing search for scientific consensus), and then observe the influence of such beliefs on subsequent reporting.

We might also conduct laboratory experiments with students, perhaps comparing the judgments of journalism students with those of non-journalism majors. Such experiments could be of value, both for those interested in developing a cognitive psychology of journalism and also for those who train future journalists.

It would also be desirable to elicit journalists' participation in laboratory experiments conducted on-site (perhaps using computer-automated procedures) at professional meetings.

Finally, in an effort to understand some of the expert-novice differences we have proposed here, it could be of great interest to compare the mental processes of student journalists with those of professionals.

Undoubtedly, as we examine newswork from a cognitive perspective, we will discover that the cognitive models developed in psychologists' laboratories do not exactly fit what goes on in the newsroom. By specifying the ways these models do not fit, we will continue to modify them; the revised models can then be tested experimentally.

Chapter X

Summary and Conclusions

Journalists are among our most visible processors of information. What reporters and editors do with the many bits of information that come their way each day is a matter of great interest both to those who produce the news and to those who consume it.

Until recently, the bulk of research devoted to understanding newsmaking has emphasized environmental influences on the process, to the neglect of cognitive influences.

In a preliminary effort to correct this oversight, we have reviewed an area of cognitive psychology that we believe offers important insights to those interested in understanding how the news media construct their versions of reality. In the process, we have speculated about how cognitive biases and errors might creep into journalists' work as they categorize people and events; theorize about them; select and question sources; select, evaluate, and recall information; and integrate their evidence into a final story. We have discussed needs for research addressing our speculations, and noted where such research has already begun. We have discussed a related need for research that will examine the effects of environmental constraints on journalists' information processing. Finally, on the assumption that journalists, at least under some circumstances, may succumb to cognitive biases and errors that lead to widely accepted judgments of "error," we also have discussed the research that explores ways to eliminate or minimize such biases and errors.

In writing this monograph, we have been aware that some of our concerns[39] bear a strong resemblance to those of traditional researchers of media bias. However, it has become clear that our approach departs from traditional approaches in a number of fundamental ways.

First, whereas most traditional bias studies have assumed an objective, unbiased reality independent of perceivers, we share with contemporary sociologists the view that reality is actively constructed.

Second, whereas traditional bias studies have concerned themselves with values and attitudes, our perspective is concerned with the workings of beliefs that may or may not have to do with values and attitudes.

Third, whereas most traditional bias studies have emphasized relationships between beliefs (usually values and attitudes) and media content, our approach emphasizes relationships between beliefs and the individual steps in a journalist's cognitive process of newsgathering. The emphasis is more on the production of news than on the product.[40]

Finally, whereas traditional bias studies have tended to assume that media biases originated with individual journalists or their superiors, we have made no such assumptions. Indeed, as we interpret the cognitive perspective, we share with more contemporary sociological approaches the assumption that many factors in the environment of individual journalists may shape the production of news. Just how these environmental factors play themselves out in the minds of individual journalists, how they influence the normal biasing processes involved in journalists' thinking, is one of many questions that we have come to regard as fascinating.

Obviously, studying journalists' thinking from a contemporary cognitive perspective will not be easy. Cognitions are not directly observable, and cognitive processes often operate well below the level of consciousness. It may also be harder to study journalists' cognitive behavior than it is to study that of their readers and audiences. Studying journalists' behavior has always been difficult, and studying their cognitive processing is more challenging still.[41]

But realization of the problems should not blind us to the possibilities for enriching studies of newsmaking. In other areas of mass media studies, cognitive models have begun to have enormous impact (Reeves, Chaffee, & Tims, 1982). In particular, cognitive models have begun to transform the study of mass media effects. Among other things, they have prompted us to revise the assumption that audiences are passive, allowing us to see that the people play a much larger role than was originally realized. They have helped us to understand more precisely how certain general characteristics of audience members, such as demographic factors, create individual differences in audience responses to media (Gunter, 1987). Finally, they have helped us to identify new questions, and have offered plausible explanations for old findings.

Although there no doubt are critical differences between audiences and journalists, it is intriguing to think that cognitive models might provoke reassessments in newswork studies as well. Conceivably, they could revise prevailing assumptions about journalists as relatively passive players within newsmaking organizations. They might help us to understand more precisely how general communicator characteristics influence the production of news. Or, as we have noted, they might prompt us to explore more precisely how a host of environmental factors come to have their effects. At the very least, they could help us to identify new questions, and offer plausible (and testable) alternative explanations for old findings.

Whether or not these things will happen is unclear. One thing, however, seems certain: the contemporary cognitive perspective will *not* have an effect unless investigators of newswork see its potential.

Endnotes

1. Anonymous, 1987.

2. Of course, just as one cannot fully understand environmental factors without understanding the mediating role of cognitions, it is also true (as van Dijk also points out) that one cannot understand the cognitive functioning of individuals without understanding environmental factors. The extent to which journalists' behavior (including their information processing) is influenced by environmental factors or by factors unique to the individual is a separate empirical question. And, impressions of environmental constraints notwithstanding, the verdict is not yet in. As Hirsch (1977, p. 24) has pointed out in another context, there is a need for research on the extent to which journalists base decisions on personal rather than organizational criteria.

3. It should be noted that most of the citations in this manuscript are illustrative rather than all-inclusive. Rather than putting "for example" or "*e.g.*" before each citation, we will in most cases simply put the illustrative citation(s) in parentheses.

4. While cognitive scientists share the "construction" assumption (and the attendant assumption that reality is largely if not totally subjective), they are not loath, as many contemporary sociologists seem to be, to use evaluative language when describing construction work. Indeed, as we shall see, inherent in the very words "bias" and "error," which permeate the work of cognitive scientists described here, is the notion that routine cognitive processing can lead to constructions of reality that are less than optimal. The presumed shortcomings of such constructions seem to revolve around the fact that they contain a restricted range of perspectives and/or that they contain information that conflicts with widely shared agreements about what is "out there" in the world.

5.   Indeed, an entire volume could be devoted to the ways that such shortcuts and routines help people function in an information-rich environment.

6.   Murray and Scanlan (1986), for example, offer a six-stage model: assign, collect, focus, order, develop, clarify. Grey (1972) offers a simple hierarchical model: pre-writing, writing, rewriting and editing, finished product (each with subtasks). Fishman (1980), in a more cognitive fashion, lists event detection, interpretation of events as meaningful, investigation of factual character of events, assembling information into stories. Parsigian (1988), in what may be the only systematically derived description of individual journalists' tasks, has concluded that journalists' activities correspond to the tasks of scientists; that is, journalists state a problem, background the problem, design a data collection strategy, collect, code and analyze data, draw conclusions, and write.

7.   News selection may be considered a cognitive task in its own right, but since news selection has received generous attention by mass communication researchers, we will not focus on that here; instead, we will concentrate on cognitive tasks more frequently associated with news treatment. Those interested in pursuing the application of a contemporary cognitive perspective to the study of news selection are referred to Kennamer (1988).

8.   The chart is adapted from Hastie and Carlston (1980), and the reader is referred there for a more complete description of system processes.

9.   It would be entirely too large a task to survey in this paper all the research on human cognition. An enormous amount of research has flowed out of the cognitive tradition in the last 15 to 20 years, much of it too esoteric for ready translation into our field.

10.   Such preferences should not be confused with motivationally based preferences posited many years ago by cognitive consistency theorists; contemporary cognitive psychologists have found systemically based preferences (which may interact with motivational factors) far more compelling. For more discussion on this point, see Fiske and Taylor, 1984.

11. It is important to stress that cognitive constructions, while not *necessarily* independent of values and attitudes and other affect-laden concepts, may be independent of them.

12. Tuchman interprets the event in sociological terms.

13. For one review of research on conformational tendencies, presented in the context of scientific hypothesis-testing, see Tweney, Dogherty and Mynatt, 1981; see also Snyder, 1984, for a more general discussion of how beliefs tend to create their own realities.

14. It should be pointed out that this is not true for all research in which subjects have been given free rein to develop their own questions. In other research (reviewed in Snyder, 1984), subjects given free rein developed confirmatory questions.

15. Put another way, they may treat what ought to be hypotheses (beliefs that are tentatively held) as assumptions (beliefs held without question). (These definitions are from Snyder, 1984). We will discuss hypotheses and assumptions more directly later, when reviewing research that has begun to explore hypothesis-confirming biases in journalism.

16. It would appear that the raised question with denials of guilt, like quotation marks and other journalistic practices identified by Tuchman (1972), may be employed in an effort to "objectify" journalistic accounts and so ward off legal challenges.

17. The fact that they confirmed the observation later does not mean that they, like Woodward and Bernstein, did attend to Nixon's hands; it is entirely possible, as we shall see when we discuss memory biases, that they did not attend to them, but later, under questioning, constructed a "memory" of them.

18. We may also identify this as a confirmation bias in which behaviors are labeled in ways that are consistent with one's *a priori* hypotheses about the person's likely competencies.

19. Patterning is hope for parents of brain-damaged child. (1985, September 8). *Sunday Herald-Times*, (Bloomington, IN) pp. E-1, E-8.

20. Donohue, *et al*. discuss this tendency in the context of a "guard dog" role of the press in which the news media are "generally conditioned to protect not one specific actor, but a structure" (p. 17).

21. Snyder (1984) explains why this might be so, and points to additional research by himself and others which is supportive of the original findings.

22. Personal communication, 1988.

23. This definition is adapted from Snyder, 1984.

24. Most of the hypotheses were descriptive in nature (such as the belief that the city's no-smoking ordinance may not be working). Other hypotheses, though, were evaluative (such as the belief that a particular fee structure for developers may not be appropriate for the community). The descriptive/evaluative distinction is one that used to be popular in psychology (*e.g.*, Jastrow, 1927). Although it is less so now, for our purposes it is a valuable distinction that may eventually allow us to link the psychological literatures concerning hypothesis-testing more directly to that concerning attitude-behavior relations.

25. This definition is also adapted from Snyder, 1984.

26. Snyder (1988). Personal communication.

27. It must be noted, however, that this particular reporter was highly experienced, and spent more than the usual amount of time on the story, which ran as a "perspective" piece on the cover of a special section. With a less experienced reporter, spending less time, this might not have been the case.

28. The information in parentheses is information that is contained in Parsigian's interview guide.

29. Personal communication, 1988.

30. It was reported as 20 years in the story, for the man requested that the number of years be disguised to protect his identity.

31. As noted in an earlier endnote, journalists' specific hypotheses and assumptions about story subjects can be either descriptive or eval-

uative, although, not surprisingly (given journalistic norms relating to objectivity), descriptive beliefs appear to be preferred.

32. As we have seen, this was (from the perspective of some sources and some social scientists) an incorrect inference. Indeed there is reason to think that such inferences by journalists may often be incorrect. In an exploratory study of what news sources do when they dislike what is said about them, Pritchard (1987) found that news sources are more likely to "lump it" than they are to complain, when the press has written something about them that they judge to be in error.

33. We have tended to focus on print media in this manuscript because that is what we know best. But obviously the technological constraints imposed on broadcast journalists are formidable, and if anything, might be expected to have an even greater effect on cognitive bias.

34. The investigators define pluralistic communities as ones "with more diversely distributed power structures and more factions with competing interests" (Olien *et al.*, 1989, p. 12).

35. It should be pointed out that Hallin does not talk about "positive" or "negative" consensus; instead, he talks about the spheres of "consensus" and "deviance" which people and perspectives occupy. Both of his spheres, however, involve consensus, which is why they are discussed this way here.

36. The word "perceived" is important here. Research has shown that people often perceive more consensus than exists. This tendency to overestimate the typicality of one's beliefs and behavior is known as the "false consensus" effect and is discussed in more detail in Fiske and Taylor (1984).

37. These people and perspectives occupy what Hallin calls the "sphere of legitimate controversy."

38. The authors are grateful to John McManus for inspiring these speculations. Personal communication, 1989.

39. We are referring to our concerns about confirmation bias.

40. In that sense, this approach is in keeping with the recent "process" emphasis in the teaching of journalism. (See Fry, 1986; Clark, 1986; Murray & Scanlan, 1983, 1986).

41. Van Dijk (1988a) discusses some of the problems he personally encountered in gaining cooperation from journalists.

References

Abelson, R. P. (1981). The psychological status of the script concept. *American Psychologist, 36,* 715-729.

Abelson, R. P., & Lalljee, M. (1987). Knowledge structures and causal explanation. In D. Hilton (Ed.), *Contemporary science and natural explanation: Commonsense conceptions of causality* (pp. 175-203). Brighton, NY: New York University Press.

Anderson, C. A. (1983). Abstract and concrete data in the perseverance of social theories: When weak data lead to unshakeable beliefs. *Journal of Experimental Social Psychology, 19,* 93-108.

Bell, B. B., & Loftus, E. F. (1989). Trivial persuasion in the courtroom. *Journal of Personality and Social Psychology, 56,* 669-679.

Belleza, F. S., & Bower, G. H. (1981). Person stereotypes and memory for people. *Journal of Personality and Social Psychology, 41,* 856-865.

Benjamin, B. (1988). *Fair play: CBS, General Westmoreland, and how a television documentory went wrong.* New York: Harper & Row.

Bernstein, C., & Woodward, R. (1974). *All the President's men.* New York: Simon and Schuster.

Black, J. B., Galambos, J. A., & Read, S. J. (1984). Comprehending stories and social situations. In R. S. Wyer & T. K. Srull (Eds.), *Handbook of social cognition* (pp. 45-86). Hillsdale, NJ: Erlbaum.

Blundell, W. E. (1986). *Storytelling step by step: A guide to better feature writing.* New York: Dow Jones.

Blundell, W. E. (1988). *The Art and Craft of Feature Writing: Based on The Wall Street Journal Guide.* New York: New American Library.

Bower, G. H. (Ed.). (1974). *The psychology of learning and motivation.* New York: Academic Press.

Bower, G. H., Black, J. B., & Turner, T. J. (1979). Scripts in memory for text. *Cognitive Psychology, 11*, 177-220.

Boyer, J. H. (1981). How editors view objectivity. *Journalism Quarterly, 58*, 24-28.

Branscombe, N. R. (1989, May). Involvement, complexity, and the use of heuristics in social judgment. Invited presentation at the Midwestern Psychological Association, Chicago.

Bransford, J. D., & Franks, J. J. (1971). The abstraction of linguistic ideas. *Cognitive Psychology, 2*, 331-350.

Breed, W. (1955). Social control in the newsroom: A functional analysis. *Social Forces, 33*, 326-335.

Cantor, N., & Mischel, W. (1977). Traits as prototypes: Effects on recognition memory. *Journal of Personality and Social Psychology, 35*, 38-48.

Chapman, L. J., & Chapman, J. P. (1969). Illusory correlation as an obstacle to the use of valid psychodiagnostic signs. *Journal of Abnormal Psychology, 14*, 271-280.

Chi, M. T. H., & Glaser, R. (1979, April). Encoding process characteristics of experts and novices in physics. Paper presented at the American Educational Research Association, San Francisco.

Chomsky, N. (1985). Beyond the bounds of unthinkable thought. *The Progressive, 49*, 28-31.

Clark, L. F., & Woll, S. B. (1981). Stereotype biases: A reconstructive analysis of their role in reconstructive memory. *Journal of Personality and Social Psychology, 41*, 1064-1072.

Clark, R. P. (1986). On writing, coaching and the Lamaze method. *APME News, 159*, 17-19.

Combs, B., & Slovic, P. (1979). Newspaper coverage of causes of death. *Journalism Quarterly, 56*, 837-843.

Crouse, T. (1973). *The boys on the bus.* New York: Ballantine.

Croxton, J. S., Eddy, T., & Morrow, N. (1984). Memory biases in the reconstruction of interpersonal encounters. *Journal of Social and Clinical Psychology, 2,* 348-354.

Darley, J. M., & Gross, P. H. (1983). A hypothesis-confirming bias in labeling effects. *Journal of Personality and Social Psychology, 44,* 20-33.

DeFrank, T. M. (1987, July 13). Not with a bang. *Newsweek,* p. 14.

"A Dole in the 'fast track'!" (1987, June 15). *Newsweek,* p. 7.

Donohue, G. A., Olien, C. N., & Tichenor, P. J. (1987, August). A "guard dog" conception of mass media. Paper presented at the Association for Education in Journalism and Mass Communication, San Antonio.

Donohue, G. A., Tichenor, P. J., & Olien, C. N. (1989). Media and protest. In L. Grunig and J. Grunig, (Eds.), *Environmental activism revisited. Monographs in environmental education and environmental studies* (Vol. 5) (pp. 22-39). Troy, OH: North American Association for Environmental Education.

Duncan, S. L. (1976). Differential social perception and attribution of intergroup violence: Testing the lower limits of stereotyping of blacks. *Journal of Personality and Social Psychology, 34,* 590-598.

Dunwoody, S. (1981). The science writing inner club: A communication link between science and the lay public. In G. C. Wilhoit & H. deBock, (Eds.), *Mass communication review yearbook* (Vol. 2) (pp. 351-359). Beverly Hills, CA: Sage.

Einhorn, H. J., & Hogarth, R. M. (1982). *A theory of diagnostic inference: II. Judging causality.* (Technical Report). Graduate School of Business Center for Decision Research, University of Chicago.

Elliott, P. (1972). *The making of a television series—A case study in the production of culture.* London: Constable.

Epstein, E. J. (1973). *News from nowhere: Television and the news.* New York: Random House.

Ericsson, K. A., & Simon, H. A. (1984). *Protocol analysis: Verbal reports as data.* Cambridge, MA: The MIT Press.

Estes, W. K. (Ed.). (1975). *Handbook of learning and cognitive processes.* (Vol. 1). Hillsdale, NJ: Erlbaum.

Ettema, J. S., & Glasser, T. L. (1985). On the epistemology of investigative journalism. *Communications, 8,* 183-206.

Fazio, R. (1986). How do attitudes guide behavior? In R. M. Sorrentino & E. T. Higgins, (Eds.), *Handbook of motivation and cognition* (pp. 204-243). New York: Guilford.

Fazio, R. H., & Herr, P. M. (1984). On the role of selective perception in the attitude-behavior process. Unpublished manuscript, Indiana University, Bloomington, IN.

Fazio, R. H., Powell, M. C., & Herr, P. M. (1983). Toward a process model of the attitude-behavior relation: Accessing one's attitude upon mere observation of the attitude object. *Journal of Personality and Social Psychology, 44,* 723-735.

Fico, F. (1984a). A comparison of legislative sources in newspaper and wire service stories. *Newspaper Research Journal, 5,* 35-44.

Fico, F. (1984b). Newspaper coverage of parttime and fulltime legislatures. *Newspaper Research Journal, 6,* 49-57.

Fischhoff, B., & Beyth, R. (1975). "I knew it would happen": Remembered probabilities of once future things. *Organizational Behavior and Human Performance, 13,* 1-16.

Fischhoff, B., Slovic, P., & Lichtenstein, S. (1977). Knowing with certainty: The appropriateness of extreme confidence. *Journal of Experimental Psychology: Human Perception and Performance, 3,* 552-564.

Fishman, M. (1980). *Manufacturing the news.* Austin: University of Texas Press.

Fiske, S. T., & Kinder, D. R. (1981). Involvement, expertise, and schema use: Evidence from political cognition. In N. Cantor & J. Kihlstrom (Eds.), *Personality, cognition and social interaction* (pp. 171-190). Hillsdale, NJ: Erlbaum.

Fiske, S. T., Kinder, D., & Larter, W. M. (1983). The novice and the expert: Knowledge-based strategies in political cognition. *Journal of Experimental and Social Psychology, 19,* 381-400.

Fiske, S. T., & Pavelchak, M. A. (1986). Category-based versus piecemeal-based affective responses: Developments in schema-triggered affect. In R. M. Sorrentino & E. T. Higgins, (Eds.), *Handbook of motivation and cognition* (pp. 167-203). New York: Guilford.

Fiske, S. T., & Taylor, S. E. (1984). *Social cognition.* Reading, MA: Addison-Wesley.

Foersterling, F., & Groenvald, A. (1983). Attributions for election results: A study of attributional hypothesis in a field study of Lower Saxony community elections (in German). *Zeitschrift für Socialpsychologie, 14,* 262-269.

Franklin, J. (1987). Myths of literary journalism: A practitioner's perspective. *Journalism Educator, 44,* 8-13.

Fry, D. (1986). The difference between editing and coaching. *APME News, 159,* 17-19.

Gandy, O. H., Jr. (1982). *Beyond agenda-setting: Information subsidies and public policy.* Norwood, NJ: Ablex.

Gans, H. J. (1980). *Deciding what's news: A study of CBS Evening News, NBC Nightly News, Newsweek and Time.* New York: Vintage.

Gilbert, D. T., & Jones, E. E. (1986). Perceiver-induced constraint: Interpretations of self-generated reality. *Journal of Personality and Social Psychology, 50,* 269-280.

Gilovich, T. (1981). Seeing the past in the present: The effect of associations to familiar events on judgments and decisions. *Journal of Personality and Social Psychology, 40,* 797-808.

Gitlin, T. (1980). *The whole world is watching: Mass media in the making and unmaking of the new left.* Berkeley, CA: University of California Press.

Graber, D. (1988). *Processing the news: How people tame the information tide* (2nd ed.). New York: Longman.

Graesser, A. C., & Black, J. B. (1985). *The psychology of questions.* Hillsdale, NJ: Erlbaum.

Graesser, A. C., Woll, S. B., Kowalski, D. J., & Smith, D. A. (1980). Memory for typical and atypical actions in scripted activities. *Journal of Experimental Psychology: Human Learning and Memory, 6,* 503-515.

Grey, D. L. (1972). *The writing process: A behavioral approach to communicating information and ideas.* Belmont, CA: Wadsworth.

Gross, P. H., & Darley, J. M. (in review). The reversal of standard stereotype effects. *Journal of Personality and Social Psychology.*

Gunter, B. (1987). *Poor reception: Misunderstanding and forgetting broadcast news.* Hillsdale, NJ: Erlbaum.

Hallin, D. (1989). *The uncensored war: The media in Vietnam.* Berkeley: University of California Press.

Hamill, R., Wilson, T. D., & Nisbett, R. E. (1980). Insensitivity to sample bias: Generalizing from atypical cases. *Journal of Personality and Social Psychology, 39,* 578-589.

Hamilton, D. L., & Gifford, R. K. (1976). Illusory correlation in interpersonal perception: A cognitive basis of stereotypic judgments. *Journal of Experimental Social Psychology, 12,* 392-407.

Hastie, R., & Carlston, D. (1980). Theoretical issues in person memory. In R. Hastie, T. M. Ostrom, E. B. Ebbesen, R. S. Wyer, D. L. Hamilton, & D. E. Carlston (Eds.), *Person memory: The cognitive basis of social perception* (pp. 1-53). Hillsdale, NJ: Erlbaum.

Hastie, R., & Kumar P. A. (1979). Person memory: Personality traits as organizing principles in memory for behaviors. *Journal of Personality and Social Psychology, 37,* 25-38.

Hastie, R., Ostrom, T.M., Ebbesen, E. B., Wyer, R. S., Hamilton, D. L., & Carolson, D. E. (1980). *Person memory: The cognitive basis of social perception.* Hillsdale, NJ: Erlbaum.

Hastorf, A. H., & Cantrill, H. (1954). They saw a game: A case study. *Journal of Abnormal and Social Psychology, 97,* 399-401.

Hayden, T., & Mischel, W. (1976). Maintaining trait consistency in the resolution of behavioral inconsistency: The wolf in sheep's clothing? *Journal of Personality and Social Psychology, 44*, 109-132.

Hayes, J. R., & Flower, L. S. (1986). Writing research and the writer. *American Psychologist, 41*, 1106-1113.

Henry, W. (1983, December 12). Journalism under fire. *Time*, pp. 76-93.

Herman, E. S., & Chomsky, N. (1988). *Manufacturing consent: The political economy of the mass media.* New York: Pantheon.

Hetherington, A. (1985). *News, newspaper and television.* London: Macmillan.

Higgins, E. T., King, G. A., & Mavin, G. H. (1982). Individual construct accessibility and subjective impressions and recall. *Journal of Personality and Social Psychology, 43*, 35-47.

Higgins, E. T., Rholes, W. S., & Jones, C. R. (1977). Category accessibility and impression formation. *Journal of Experimental Social Psychology, 13*, 141-154.

Hirsch, P. M. (1977). Occupational, organizational, and institutional models in mass media research: Toward an integrated framework. In P. M. Hirsch, P. V. Miller, & K. G. Kline, (Eds.), *Strategies for communication research* (pp. 13-42). Beverly Hills, CA: Sage.

Houston, D. A., & Fazio, R. H. (1989). Biased processing as a function of attitude accessibility: Making objective judgments subjectively. *Social Cognition, 7*, 51-66.

Jastrow, J. (1927). The animus of psychical research. In C. Murchison (Ed.), *The case for and against psychical belief.* Worcester, MA: Clark University Press. Cited in Rokeach, M. (1972). *Beliefs, attitudes, and values: A theory of organization and change.* San Francisco: Jossey-Bass.

Jones, E. E. (1979). The rocky road from acts to dispositions. *American Psychologist, 64*, 300-305.

Jones, E. E., & Harris, V. A. (1967). The attribution of attitudes. *Journal of Experimental Social Psychology, 3*, 1-24

Judd, C. M., & Kulik, J. A. (1980). Schematic effects of social attitudes on information processing and recall. *Journal of Personality and Social Psychology, 38*, 569-578.

Kennamer, J. D. (1988). News values and the vividness of information. *Written Communication, 5*, 108-123.

Kruglanski, A. W. (in press). *Basic processes in social cognition: A theory of lay epistemology.* New York: Plenum.

Kruglanski, A. W., & Freund, T. (1983). The freezing and unfreezing of lay inferences: Effects on impressional primacy, ethnic stereotyping and numerical anchoring. *Journal of Experimental Social Psychology, 19*, 448-468.

Lacy, S., Fico, F., & Simon, T. (in press). The relationships among economic, newsroom and content variables. *Journal of Media Economics.*

Lalljee, M., & Abelson, R. P. (1983). The organization of explanations. In M. Hewstone, (Ed.), *Attribution theory: Social and functional extensions* (pp. 65-80). Oxford: B. Blackwell.

Larkin, S. H., McDermott, S., Simon, D. P., & Simon, H. A. (1980). Models of competence in solving physics problems. *Science, 208*, 1335-1342.

Lau, R. R. (1984). Dynamics of the attribution process. *Journal of Personality and Social Psychology, 46*, 1017-1028.

Lau, R. R., & Russell, D. (1980). Attributions in the sports pages: A field test of some current hypotheses in attribution research. *Journal of Personality and Social Psychology, 39*, 29-38.

Leary, M. R. (1982). Hindsight distortion and the 1980 Presidential election. *Personality and Social Psychology Bulletin, 8*, 257-263.

Leddo, J., Abelson, R.P., & Gross, P. H. (1984). Conjunctive explanations: When two reasons are better than one. *Journal of Personality and Social Psychology, 47*, 933-943.

Linville, P. W., & Jones, E. E. (1980). Polarized appraisals of outgroup members. *Journal of Personality and Social Psychology, 38*, 689-703.

Loftus, E. F. (1979). *Eyewitness testimony*. Cambridge, MA: Harvard University Press.

Loftus, E. F., & Palmer, J. C. (1973). Reconstruction of automobile destruction: An example of the interaction between language and memory. *Journal of Verbal Learning and Verbal Behavior, 13*, 585-589.

Lord, C. G., Lepper, M. R., & Thompson, W. C. (1980, September). Inhibiting biased assimilation in the consideration of new evidence on social policy issues. Paper presented at the meeting of the American Psychological Association, Montreal.

Lord, C. G., Ross, L., & Lepper, M. R. (1979). Biased assimilation and attitude polarization: The effects of prior theories on subsequently considered evidence. *Journal of Personality and Social Psychology, 37*, 2098-2109.

MacDougall, C. D. (1982). *Interpretative reporting* (8th ed.). New York: Macmillan.

McCombs, M. E., & Shaw, D. L. (1976). Structuring the "unseen environment." *Journal of Communication, 26*, 18-21.

Mencher, M. (1987). Journalists should find truth before search starts for beauty. *Journalism Educator, 42*, 11-17.

Meyer, P. (1987). *Ethical journalism* (pp. 191-195). White Plains, NY: Longman.

Miller, M. W. (1987, June 19). Seldom seen now, Boesky nevertheless leaves a few tracks. *The Wall Street Journal*, pp. 1, 12.

Morgan, M. P. (1989). *A study of ethics codes at the Indianapolis newspapers*. Unpublished master's thesis. Indiana University School of Journalism, Bloomington, IN.

Murray, D. M., & Scanlan, C. (1983). Process approach to newswriting. In C. Scanlan (Ed.). *How I wrote the story: A book for writers by writers about writing* (pp. 1-4) (1st ed).. Providence, RI: The Providence Journal Company.

Murray, D. M., & Scanlan, C. (1986). The process approach. In C. Scanlan (Ed.), *How I wrote the story: A book for writers by writers about writing* (pp. 3-8) (2nd ed.). Providence, RI: The Providence Journal Company.

Myers, D. G. (1987). *Social psychology* (2nd ed.). New York: McGraw-Hill.

Nelkin, D. (1987). *Selling science: How the press covers science and technology.* New York: W. H. Freeman.

Nisbett, R. E., & Borgida, E. (1975). Attribution and the psychology of prediction. *Journal of Personality and Social Psychology, 32,* 932-943.

Nisbett, R. E., & Ross, L. (1980). *Human inference: Strategies and shortcomings of social judgment.* Englewood Cliffs, NJ: Prentice Hall.

Nisbett, R. E., & Wilson, T. D. (1977). Telling more than we can know: Verbal reports on mental processes. *Psychological Review, 84,* 231-259.

Nord, D. P. (1985). The ideology of the press: Why press bias isn't what it appears to be. *The Cresset, 49,* 14-17.

Olien, C. N., Tichenor, P. J., Donohue, G. A., Sandstom, K. L., & McLeod, D. M. (1989, May). Community structure and editor opinions about planning. Paper presented to the American Association for Public Opinion Research, St. Petersburg, FL.

Parsigian, E. K. (1988). News reporting: Method in the midst of chaos. *Journalism Quarterly, 64,* 721-730.

Pitts, B. J. (1982). Protocol analysis of the newswriting process. *Newspaper Research Journal, 4,* 12-21.

Read, S. J. (1986). Constructing causal scenarios: A knowledge structure approach to causal reasoning. Unpublished manuscript, University of Southern California.

Reeves, B., Chaffee, S. H., & Tims, A. (1982). Social cognition and mass communication research. In M. E. Roloff & C. R. Berger (Eds.), *Social cognition and communication* (pp. 287-326). Beverly Hills, CA: Sage.

Rogoff, B., & Lave, J. (1984). *Everyday cognition: Its development in social context.* Cambridge, MA: Harvard University Press.

Rosch, E., & Lloyd, B. B. (Eds.). (1978). *Cognition and categorization.* Hillsdale, NJ: Erlbaum.

Ross, L. (1977). The intuitive psychologist and his shortcomings: Distortions in the attribution process. In L. Berkowitz, (Eds.), *Advances in experimental social psychology* (Vol. 10) (pp. 174-220). New York: Academic Press.

Ross, L. D., Amabile, T. M., & Steinmetz, J. L. (1977). Social roles, social control, and biases in social perception processes. *Journal of Personality and Social Psychology, 35,* 485-494.

Ross, L., Lepper, M. R., & Hubbard, M. (1975). Perseverance in self-perception and social perception: Biased attribution processes in the debriefing paradigm. *Journal of Personality and Social Psychology, 32,* 880-892.

Ross, M., McFarland, C., & Fletcher, G. S. O. (1981). The effect of attitude on the recall of personal histories. *Journal of Personality and Social Psychology, 10,* 627-634.

Rumelhart, D. E., & Ortony, A. (1977). The representation of knowledge in memory. In R. C. Anderson, R. J. Spiro, & W. E. Montague, (Eds.), *Schooling and the acquisition of knowledge* (pp. 99-135). Hillsdale, NJ: Erlbaum.

Schneider, W., & Shiffrin, R. M. (1977). Controlled and automatic human information processing: I. Detection, search, and attention. *Psychological Review, 84,* 1-66.

Shaklee, H., & Fischoff, B. (1977). *Discounting multicausal attribution: The principle of minimal causation* (Report No. 77-11). Eugene, OR: Decision Research.

Shank, R. C., & Abelson, R. P. (1977). *Scripts, plans, goals and understanding.* Hillsdale, NJ: Erlbaum.

Shiffrin, R. M., & Schneider, W. (1977). Controlled and automatic human information processing: II. Perceptual learning, automatic attending, and general theory. *Psychological Review, 84,* 127-190.

Shoemaker, P. J. (1987). Building a theory of news content: A synthesis of current approaches. *Journalism Monographs*, No. 103.

Sigelman, L. (1973). Reporting the news: An organizational analysis. *American Journal of Sociology, 79*, 132-151.

Sims, H., & Gioia, D. A. & Associates. (1986). *The thinking organization.* San Francisco: Jossey-Bass.

Slovic, P. (1986). Informing and educating the public about risk. *Risk Analysis, 6*, 403-415.

Slovic, P. & Fischoff, B. (1977). On the psychology of experimental surprises. *Journal of Experimental Psychology: Human Perception and Performance, 3*, 544-551.

Smith, D. A, & Graesser, A. C. (1981). Memory for actions in scripted activities as a function of typicality, retention interval, and retrieval task. *Memory and Cognition, 9*, 550-559.

Smith, E. E., & Meadin, D. L. (1981). *Categories and concepts.* Cambridge, MA: Harvard University Press.

Snyder, M. (1984). When belief creates reality. *Advances in Experimental Social Psychology, 18*, 247-305.

Snyder, M., & Cantor, N. (1979). Testing hypotheses about other people: The use of historical knowledge. *Journal of Experimental Social Psychology, 15*, 330-342.

Snyder, M., & Gangestad, S. (1981). Hypothesis-testing processes. In J. H. Harvey, W. Ickes, & R. F. Kidd, (Eds.), *New directions in attribution research* (pp. 171-195) Hillsdale, NJ: Erlbaum.

Snyder, M., & Swann, W. B., Jr. (1978). Hypothesis-testing processes in social interaction. *Journal of Personality and Social Psychology, 36*, 1202-1212.

Snyder, M., Tanke, E. D., & Bersheid, E. (1977). Social perception and interpersonal behavior: On the self-fulfilling nature of social stereotypes. *Journal of Personality and Social Psychology, 35*, 656-666.

Snyder, M., & Uranowitz, S. W. (1978). Reconstructing the past: Some cognitive consequences of person perception. *Journal of Personality and Social Psychology, 36*, 941-950.

Society of Professional Journalists/Sigma Delta Chi. (1987). Code of Ethics.

Stevenson, R. L., & Greene, M. T. (1980). A reconsideration of bias in the news. *Journalism Quarterly, 57*, 115-121.

Stocking, S. H. (1989a). Applications of cognitive psychology to environmental communication: Toward a cognitive psychology of journalism. In L. Grunig & J. Grunig (Eds.), *Environmental activism revisited.* Monographs in environmental education and environmental studies (Vol. V) (pp. 125-137). Troy, OH: North American Association for Environmental Education.

Stocking, S. H. (1989b, May). Processing the news: Toward a cognitive psychology of journalism. Invited presentation to Midwestern Psychological Association, Chicago.

Stocking, S. H., & LaMarca, N. (1989, May). How journalists describe their stories: Hypotheses and assumptions in newsmaking. Paper presented to the Mass Communication Division, International Communication Association, San Francisco.

Swann, W. B., Jr., Giulano, T., & Wegner, D. M. (1982). Where leading questions can lead: The power of conjecture in social interaction. *Journal of Personality and Social Psychology, 42*, 1025-1035.

Swann, W. B., Jr., & Snyder, M. (1980). On translating beliefs into action: Theories of ability and their application in an instructional setting. *Journal of Personality and Social Psychology, 38*, 879-888.

Tankard, J. (1976). Reporting and the scientific method. In M. McCombs, D. L. Shaw, D. Grey (Eds.), *Handbook of reporting methods* (pp. 51-52). Boston: Houghton Mifflin.

Taylor, S. E. (1981). A categorization approach to stereotyping. In D. L. Hamilton (Ed.), *Cognitive processes in stereotyping and intergroup behavior.* (pp. 83-114). Hillsdale, NJ: Erlbaum.

Taylor, S. E., & Crocker, J. (1981). Schematic bases of social information processing. In E. T. Higgins, C. D. Herman, & M. P. Zanna (Eds.), *Social cognition: The Ontario symposium* (Vol. 1) (pp. 89-134). Hillsdale, NJ: Erlbaum.

Taylor, S. E., & Thompson, S.C. (1982). Stalking the elusive "vividness" effect. *Psychological Review, 89*, p.155-181.

Tichenor, P. J., Donohue, G. A., & Olien, C. N. (1980). *Community conflict and the press.* Beverly Hills, CA: Sage.

Trillin, C. (1986, February 17). Covering the cops. *The New Yorker*, pp. 39-57.

Trope, Y., & Bassok, M. (1982). Confirmatory and diagnosing strategies in social information gathering. *Journal of Personality and Social Psychology, 43*, 22-34.

Tuchman, G. (1978). *Making news: A study in the construction of reality.* New York: The Free Press.

Tuchman, G. (1972). Objectivity as a strategic ritual: An examination of newsmen's notions of objectivity. *American Journal of Sociology, 77*, 660-679.

Tversky, A., & Kahneman, D. (1978). Causal schemata in judgments under uncertainty. In M. Fishbein (Ed.), *Progress in social psychology* (pp. 49-72). Hillsdale, NJ: Erlbaum.

Tversky, A., & Kahneman, D. (1974). Judgment under uncertainty: Heuristics and biases. *Science, 185*, 1124-1131.

Tweney, R. D., Dogherty, M., & Mynatt, C. R. (Eds.). (1981). *On scientific thinking.* New York: Columbia University Press.

van Dijk, T. A. (1983). Discourse analysis: Its development and application to the structure of news. *Journal of Communication, 33*, 20-43.

van Dijk, T. A. (1988a). *News discourse.* Hillsdale, NJ: Erlbaum.

van Dijk, T. A. (1988b). *News analysis: Case studies of international and national news in the press: Lebanon, ethnic minorities and squatters.* Hillsdale, NJ: Erlbaum.

VanSlyke Turk, J. (1986). Information subsidies and media content: A study of public relations influence on the news. *Journalism Monographs,* No. 100.

Wason, P. C., & Johnson-Laird, P. N. (1965). *Psychology of reasoning: Structure and content.* London: Batsford.

Wearden, S. T. (1987, August). Attitudes of North Carolina legislators and statehouse reporters regarding the use of anonymous sources—A coorientation study. Paper presented to the Communication Theory and Methodology Division of the Association for Education in Journalism and Mass Communication, San Antonio, TX.

Weaver, D. H., & Wilhoit, G. C. (1986). *The American journalist: A portrait of U.S. news people and their work.* Bloomington, IN: Indiana University Press.

Whitney, D. C. (1982). Mass communicator studies: Similarity, difference, and level of analysis. In J. S. Ettema & D. C. Whitney (Eds.), *Individuals in mass media organizations: Creativity and constraint* (pp. 241-254). Beverly Hills, CA: Sage.

Wiener, B. (1985). "Spontaneous" causal thinking. *Psychological Bulletin, 97,* 74-84.

Weir, D., & Noyes, D. (1983). *Raising hell: How the Center for Investigative Reporting gets the story.* Reading, MA: Addison-Wesley.

White, D. M. (1950). The gatekeeper: A case study in the selection of news. *Journalism Quarterly, 27,* 383-390.

Wilder, D. A., & Allen, V. L. (1978). Group membership and preference for information about others. *Personality and Social Psychology Bulletin, 4,* 106-110.

Wilhoit, G. C., & Weaver, D. H. (1980). *Newsroom guide to polls & surveys.* Washington, DC: American Newspaper Publishers Association.

Wyer, R. S., Jr. (1974). *Cognitive organization and change: An information processing approach.* Potomac, MD: Erlbaum.

Wyer Jr., R. S., & Gordon, S. E. (1982). The recall of information about persons and groups. *Journal of Experimental Social Psychology, 18,* 128-164.

Wyer, R. S., Jr., Srull, T. K., Gordon, S. E., & Hartwick, J. (1982). Effects of processing objectives on the recall of prose material. *Journal of Personality and Social Psychology, 43,* 674-688.

Appendix

For the uninitiated, it may be instructive to provide a simplified schematic model of the human cognitive system as psychologists currently understand it. (A more detailed description of the human information processing system can be found in Hastie, Ostrom, Ebbessen, Wyer, Hamilton, & Carlston, 1980; Estes, 1975; Bower, 1974; and Wyer, 1974).

Most cognitive psychologists would agree, based on an expanding body of supportive evidence, that the human information processing system consists of two memory centers—a short-term store and a long-term store.

Short-term memory, often referred to as "working memory," primarily holds on to the information taken in from the immediate environment. It consists of the information under current consideration—what the individual is making sense of at this moment (thus, its designation as "working" memory). The individual may experience activity in this short-term work center as focused attention. As noted, the capacity of this short-term store is limited. Thus, within this system we may find selection processes that work to bring certain pieces of information into working memory, leaving out others. Some of the information from short-term storage will be guided into long-term storage centers. It is within these long-term centers that we store the information we typically think of as our world knowledge.

Our accumulated knowledge is stored in categories. The precise nature of the representation of information in these categories, and the larger organizational structure of categories, is the subject of much current debate (see Rosch & Lloyd, 1978; Smith & Meadin, 1981). However, it can be said that in general people have categories containing their knowledge of objects (chairs, cats), and of events in the world and their unfolding (referred to as "scripts"), and categories which contain knowledge about individual others or social groups (referred to as "schemas"

111

or "stereotypes"). The category representation may include the attributes of the event, person, or group, and in some cases, information about the causes and consequences of events or people's behavior (Rumelhart & Ortony, 1977; Abelson, 1981). Although specific examples of event types may also be included in the category representation, the cognitive category is not simply a collection of examples or events or people, but rather represents the shared features of events in a more abstract way (Rosch & Lloyd, 1978; Smith & Meadin, 1981).

Some of our categories will be simple and sparse, and others will be quite complex and elaborate (Linville & Jones, 1980; Fiske & Kinder, 1981). Thus a category containing one's knowledge about New Zealanders may contain only the attributes "island dwellers," or "English-speaking." Our categories containing knowledge of the process of giving birth may be quite elaborate, containing numerous features of the gestation period and information about the causal unfolding of the process. Categories used in the understanding of news events may be similarly simple or complex.

Incoming information from the world may be added to these categories (learning) and information from the categories stored in long-term memory may be taken out and used to make sense of incoming information contained in short-term memory (understanding or comprehension). The two storage centers are closely tied, and are interactive.

In addition to storage centers, the human cognitive system is assumed to include sets of processes that allow us to interact with the outside world. This interaction is first accomplished by perceiving and taking in information and bringing the information into focused attention. These tasks, which enter stimuli into working memory, are referred to as encoding.

Additional processes make it possible for the individual to comprehend the encoded information. These processes include simple retrieval processes in which information from our categories is pulled out to help us understand the stimuli under current consideration (categorization), and more complex tasks that involve assessing the causes or consequences of what is taken in. These include organizing and evaluating the information, elaborating on the incoming information, and selecting

112

out aspects of the encoded stimulus array to be placed in long-term storage until recalled for later use.

It is important to note that these processes or system tasks are dependent on the nature and limitations of the storage centers. Moreover, and of considerable importance, information from the storage centers (schemas, scripts, stereotypes, and all other types of category-based information) will exert a guiding influence on the processing tasks (Taylor & Crocker, 1981; Fiske & Taylor, 1984).

Name Index

A

Abelson, R. P.	8, 9, 45
Allen, V. L.	78
Amabile, T. M.	48
Anderson, C. A.	36, 77

B

Bassok, M.	30, 78
Bell, B. B.	42
Belleza, F. S.	51
Benjamin, B.	32
Bentsen, Lloyd	53
Bernstein, Carl	24, 38, 91
Bersheid, E.	31
Beyth, R.	52
Black, J. B.	16, 45
Blundell, W. E.	19-21, 61, 74
Boesky, Ivan	37
Borgida, E.	41
Bower, G. H.	16, 45, 51
Boyer, J. H.	58, 73
Branscombe, N. R.	78
Bransford, J. D.	16
Breed, W.	2, 70
Buchanan, Edna	34
Bush, George	53

C

Cantor, N.	16, 30
Cantrill, H.	38
Carlston, D.	7, 90
Carter, Jimmy	52
Castro, Fidel	48
Chaffee, S. H.	86
Chapman, J. P.	46
Chapman, L. J.	46
Chi, M. T. H.	23

Chomsky, N.	2, 75
Clark, L. F.	51
Clark, R. P.	94
Combs, B.	43, 69
Cronkite, Walter	1
Crouse, T.	2, 15
Croxton, J. S.	51

D

Darley, J. M.	36, 38, 78
DeFrank, T. M.	14
Dogherty, M.	91
Dole, Elizabeth	34
Dole, Robert	34
Donohue, G. A.	2, 15, 49, 92
Duncan, S. L.	14
Dunwoody, S.	2, 15

E

Einhorn, H. J.	45
Elliott, P.	28
Epstein, E. J.	2
Ericsson, K. A.	80
Ervin, Sam	29
Ettema, J. S.	60, 64, 65

F

Fazio, R.	23, 37, 38
Ferraro, Geraldine	40
Fico, F.	71
Fischhoff, B.	47, 52, 79
Fishman, M.	2, 15, 28, 36, 81, 90
Fiske, S. T.	23, 24, 36, 39 43, 90, 93
Flower, S. S.	80
Foat, Ginny	34
Foersterling, F.	60, 79
Franklin, J.	19

Franks, J. J.	16
Freund, T.	53
Fry, D.	94

G

Galambos, J. A.	45
Gallup, G.	1
Gandy, O. H.	71
Gangestad, S.	59
Gans, H. J.	15, 61, 81
Gifford, R. K.	46
Gilbert, D. T.	48
Gilovich, T.	17
Gioia, D. A.	57
Gitlin, T.	15, 81
Glaser, R.	23
Glasser, T. L.	60, 64, 65
Gordon, S. E.	17, 50
Graber, D.	60
Graesser, A. C.	16, 45
Greene, E. W.	1
Grey, D. L.	90
Groenvald, A.	60, 79
Gross, P. H.	78
Guilano, T.	33
Gunter, B.	87

H

Hallin, D.	61, 74, 93
Hamill, R.	41
Hamilton, D. L.	46
Harris, V. A.	47, 49
Hart, Gary	49
Hastie, R.	7, 37, 90
Hastorf, A. H.	38
Hayden, T.	37, 78
Hayes, J. R.	80
Hearst, Patricia	48, 49
Hearst, Randolph	48
Henry, W.	34

Herman, E. S.	2
Hetherington, A.	3
Higgins, E. T.	14, 22, 70
Hirsch, P. M.	2, 89
Hogarth, R. M.	45
Houston, D. A.	37
Hubbard, M.	37, 56, 78

J

Jackson, Jesse	40, 69
Jastrow, J.	92
Johnson-Laird, P. N.	27
Jones, C. R.	14, 22
Jones, E. E.	24, 47-49, 78
Judd, C. M.	36

K

Kahneman, D.	29, 41
Kennamer, J. D.	90
Kennedy, John F.	52
Kinder, D.	23, 24, 36
King, G. A.	22, 70
Kruglanski, A. W.	53, 54, 71
Kulik, J. A.	36

L

Lacy, S.	71
Lalljee, M.	8, 9, 45
LaMarca, N.	59, 60, 62, 81
Larkin, S. H.	23
Larter, W. M.	24
Lau, R. R.	60, 79
Lave, J.	57
Leary, M. R.	52
Leddo, J.	8, 45
Lepper, M. R.	35-38, 56, 77, 78
Linville, P. W.	24
Loftus, E. F.	38, 42, 51
Lord, C. G.	35, 36, 38, 77

M

MacDougall, C. D.	59
Mavin, G. H.	22, 70
McCombs, M. E.	2
Mencher, M.	19
Meyer, P.	68
Miller, M. W.	37
Mischel, W.	16, 37, 38
Morgan, M. P.	74
Morrow, N.	51
Murray, D. M.	90, 94
Myers, D. G.	52
Mynatt, C. R.	91

N

Nelkin, D.	39, 40, 61
Nisbett, R. E.	29, 35, 41, 81
Nixon, Richard	38, 49, 91
Nord, D. P.	2
Noyes, D.	19

O

Olien, C. N.	2, 15, 49, 62, 72, 73, 93

P

Palmer, J. C.	51
Parsigian, E. K.	54, 63, 64, 90, 92
Pavelchak, M. A.	23
Pitts, B. J.	80, 81
Powell, M. C.	23
Pritchard, D.	93

Q

Quayle, Dan	53

R

Read, S. J.	45
Reagan, Ronald	49, 52
Reeves, B.	86

Rholes, W. S.	14, 22
Rogoff, B.	57
Ross, L.	29, 35, 36, 38, 41, 48, 56, 78
Ross, M.	51
Russell, D.	60, 79

S

Scanlan, C.	90, 94
Schneider, W.	23
Shaklee, H.	47
Shank, R. C.	8, 45
Shaw, D. L.	2
Shiffrin, R. M.	23
Shoemaker, P. J.	2
Sigelman, L.	20
Simon, H. A.	80
Simon, T.	71
Sims, H.	57
Slovic, P.	43, 52, 69, 79
Smith, D. A.	16
Snyder, M.	29-31, 36, 51, 59, 91, 92
Steinmetz, J. L.	48
Stevenson, L. K.	1
Stocking, S. H.	27, 28, 59, 60, 62, 65, 67, 68, 79, 81
Swann, W. B.	29, 33, 34, 36

T

Tankard, J.	29
Tanke, E. D.	31
Taylor, S. E.	24, 39-41, 43, 90, 93
Thompson, S. C.	41
Thompson, W. C.	77
Tichenor, P. J.	2, 15, 49
Tims, A.	86
Trillin, C.	34, 39
Trope, Y.	30, 78
Tuchman, G.	2, 15, 16, 74, 81, 91
Turner, T. J.	16, 45

Tversky, A.   29, 41
Tweney, R. D.   91

U

Uranowitz, S. W.   51

V

van Dijk, T. A.   viii, 60, 72, 80, 89, 94
Van Gelder, Lindsy   16, 17, 58
VanSlyke Turk, J.   71

W

Wallace, Mike   32
Wason, P. C.   27
Weardon, S. T.   3
Weaver, D. H.   3, 29

Wegner, D. M.   33
Weir, D.   19
Westmoreland, William   32
White, D. M.   2
Whitney, D. C.   2
Wiener, B.   60
Wilder, D. A.   78
Wilhoit, G. C.   3, 29
Wilson, T. D.   41, 81
Woll, S. B.   51
Woodward, Bob   24, 38, 91
Wyer, R. S.   17, 50

Y

Yalow, Rosalyn   39, 40